Obama

On Obama examines some of the key philosophical questions that accompany the historic emergence of the 44th US president. The purpose of the book is to take seriously the once common thought that the Obama presidency had ushered in a post-historical age. Three questions organize the argument of the book: What's living and dead in the idea of post-racialism? Does Mr. Obama's preference for problem-solving over ideological warfare mark him not just as a post-partisan figure but as a philosophical pragmatist? Does the US become post-imperial when the descendants of slaves and of British imperial subjects inhabit the White House? In addition to taking up these questions, the book considers Mr. Obama's own relationship to the post-historical idea and explores the ethical implications of certain ways of entertaining that idea.

Paul C. Taylor teaches philosophy and African American studies at Pennsylvania State University, USA.

Thinking in Action

Series editors: Simon Critchley, *The New School University, USA*, and Richard Kearney, *Boston College, USA,* and *University College Dublin, Ireland*

Thinking in Action takes philosophy to its public. Each book in the series is written by a major international philosopher or thinker, engages with an important contemporary topic, and is clearly and accessibly written. The series informs and sharpens debate on issues as wide ranging as the Internet, religion, the problem of immigration and refugees, criticism, architecture, and the way we think about science. Punchy, short and stimulating, **Thinking in Action** is an indispensable starting point for anyone who wants to think seriously about major issues confronting us today.

PRAISE FOR THE SERIES

'. . . allows a space for distinguished thinkers to write about their passions.'
The Philosophers' Magazine

'. . . deserve high praise.'
Boyd Tonkin, *The Independent (UK)*

'This is clearly an important series. I look forward to receiving future volumes.'
Frank Kermode, author of *Shakespeare's Language*

'both rigorous and accessible.'
Humanist News

'the series looks superb.'
Quentin Skinner

'. . . an excellent and beautiful series.'
Ben Rogers, author of *A.J. Ayer: A Life*

'Routledge's Thinking in Action series is the theory junkie's answer to the eminently pocketable Penguin 60s series.'
Mute Magazine (UK)

'Routledge's new series, *Thinking in Action*, brings philosophers to our aid. . . .'
The Evening Standard (UK)

'. . . a welcome series by Routledge.'
Bulletin of Science, Technology and Society (Can)

'Routledge's innovative new "Thinking in Action" series takes the concept of philosophy a step further.'
The Bookwatch

PAUL C. TAYLOR

On
Obama

Routledge
Taylor & Francis Group

NEW YORK AND LONDON

First published 2016
by Routledge
711 Third Avenue, New York, NY 10017

and by Routledge
2 Park Square, Milton Park, Abingdon, Oxon OX14 4RN

Routledge is an imprint of the Taylor & Francis Group, an informa business

Library of Congress Cataloging in Publication Data
Taylor, Paul C. (Paul Christopher), 1967–
  On Obama/Paul C. Taylor.
  pages cm.—(Thinking in action)
  1. Obama, Barack. 2. United States—Politics and government—2009–
  3. Communication in politics—United States—History—21st century.
  4. Presidents—United States—Biography. 5. Post-racialism—United
  States. 6. United States—Race relations—Political aspects.
  7. United States—Social conditions—21st century. I. Title.
  E908.3.T39 2015
  973.932092–dc23
  2015016121

ISBN: 978-0-415-52546-6 (hbk)
ISBN: 978-0-415-52547-3 (pbk)
ISBN: 978-0-203-11981-5 (ebk)

Typeset in Times New Roman and DIN
by Florence Production Ltd, Stoodleigh, Devon, UK

Contents

Acknowledgements

I would like to thank Andrew Beck, Routledge's indefatigable philosophy editor, for his patience with and interest in this project. His editorial assistants Laura Briskman and John Downes-Angus have provided invaluable guidance and encouragement. Anonymous reviewers for the press gave helpful comments, as did audiences at Oberlin College, Rhodes College, and the University of Memphis. I am grateful to Meredith Gadsby, Charles McKinney, Luvell Anderson, and Charles Peterson for the opportunities to speak at those institutions, and for sharing with me their students, their colleagues, their thoughts on the project, and their expert insights into the political and philosophical issues that frame the project. Audiences at Morehouse College and SUNY-Oneonta were kind enough to discuss much earlier versions of this project with me, and encouraged me to think that there was enough in it to develop further. I am especially grateful to Karina Cespedes (now at Colorado State), Chris Keegan, and Kathleen O'Mara for their encouragement during my visit to upstate New York, and to Illya Davis and to my sister Mona Phillips for challenging conversations during my visit to Morehouse.

Mark Sanders and Colin Koopman gave me the opportunity to present what became Chapter 2 at a meeting of the Society for the Advancement of American Philosophy. Similarly, Charles Mills and Robert Gooding-Williams gave me the chance to think through what became Chapter 1 for a conference that I turned out to be unable to attend. Without the advice and support of these colleagues I would not have been able to imagine this project at all.

I benefited from edifying discussions with Eddie Glaude, Leigh Johnson, Anne Eaton, Falguni Sheth, Alphonso Grant, Judith Green, and Anika Simpson at various points along the way. And I had the benefit of advice from my wife, Wilna Julmiste, on one of the knottier problems in the project: how to relate cross-dressing, boot-licking Victorians to the Obama presidency.

Parts of Chapters 1 and 2 appear, in earlier forms, in "Is It Sometime Yet?" *Contemporary Pragmatism* 8:2 (December 2011), 17–29, and in "Taking Post-Racialism Seriously: From Movement Mythology to Racial Formation," *The Du Bois Review* 11.1 (Spring 2014).

Introduction

"We were born of change."
Barack Obama at Selma, AL (March 7, 2015)[1]

When Barack Hussein Obama became the president of the United States of America, observers around the world and across the political spectrum decided that an old era was ending and a new one was dawning. Many of these people, particularly among US conservatives, took this as an occasion for nostalgia and lamentation. Many more, particularly among US progressives and African Americans, took it as a reason for hope and celebration. But for a substantial number of both supporters and critics, Mr. Obama's election meant that things might now be *different*, in ways that would require new vocabularies, concepts, sensibilities, and practices.

The idea of a world-historical "Obama moment" no longer resonates in the way it once did. The world's determination to go on largely as before—a determination that we see playing out in the upheavals in Ferguson, Missouri, in Gaza and Ukraine, and in the halls of the US Congress—has left many of the president's supporters chastened and many of his critics encouraged. At the same time, the passage of time has given us an entire generation of people for whom Mr. Obama has been president for as long as they've been paying attention. But these empirical complications do not foreclose the philosophical questions that attend the novelty of this administration.

And make no mistake, Mr. Obama is, in many respects, an historical novelty. I do not mean by this that he is a trivial curiosity.

I mean that, as William James says, "[t]ime keeps budding into new moments, every one of which presents a content which in its individuality never was before and will never be again," and that Mr. Obama's emergence is one of these moments.[2] It is not always clear what counts as an instance of genuine novelty; this is the sort of thing that gets easier to see with the perspective of time. In this case, after the political controversies of the moment recede into the background, we will still be compelled to say things like this: Mr. Obama was the first president to identify (plausibly) as black, to reach maturity after the upheavals of the sixties, to take office after the controversial and bellicose Bush–Cheney administration, and to reckon systematically with the global consequences of a deindustrialized and hyper-financialized US economy.

This litany of firsts quickly raises a number of essentially philosophical questions. I'll focus in what follows on three such questions, and on the tensions and subsequent questions that the questions generate.

First: Does Mr. Obama's ability to seize the Oval Office, and to do so despite the legacies of US racism and his own indifference to the rituals of traditional racial politics, mean that the US has become post-racial? Or, perhaps better: how can we reconcile our short-lived enthusiasm for the idea of post-racialism with, among other things, the frequency with which black and brown people suffer and die under dubious circumstances at the hands of actors who are authorized or excused by the state? (Think here of course of Michael Brown and Eric Garner, but also of Guantanamo, and of drone strikes.)

Second: Will the multiple global crises on Mr. Obama's plate, or whatever insights he's gleaned from being descended from Afro-British colonial subjects, make him our first post-imperial president? Or, to take a different angle of approach to this question of political community: Does Mr. Obama's election in a nation built on racial slavery and expropriation mean that we have become not just post-racial but also, somehow, post-national or post-colonial? And how do we reconcile the temptations of this thought with Mr. Obama's easy acceptance of the instruments of imperial power, military, financial, and otherwise?

And third: Does Mr. Obama's preference for consensus-building over ideology, for problem-solving over partisan bickering, mark him as a post-partisan politician? Is there anything at stake in understanding this preference, as some have suggested, as a form of philosophical pragmatism? And how do we reconcile the uneven commitment to this preference—some think the commitment has waned over time, especially in the president's second term; I think it was always severely constrained—with the unquestionably inspiring expressions of it that we find in Mr. Obama's writings and speeches?

To ask these questions, as one coherently might and as many people have, is to ask whether we have, with respect to some particular set of considerations or dynamics, become post-historical. And to ask this broader question is to foreground the theoretical and philosophical assumptions behind the act of historical description. One needs a theory to identify historical episodes, and to say when they've come to a close. And one needs a philosophy of history to say, as Obama's litany of firsts has moved and still moves many of us to say, that *this* episode, the one just past, is a genuine ending, with no sequel or next act in the offing.

On Obama will articulate and examine some of the philosophic questions and assumptions that accompany the historic emergence of the 44th US president. The book will not evaluate Mr. Obama's effectiveness as a politician or statesman, nor will it check for or measure the gap between his campaign promises and his administration's policies. It will not compare his public utterances over time to determine their consistency with each other and with the facts, nor will it offer a view on the prospects for the Democratic Party, for progressive ideals, or for American global hegemony. It will eventually, after the evidence, such as it is, has been assembled, consider the broadly political implications of Mr. Obama's way of inhabiting the presidency—"broadly political" in a sense that has to do with the condition of the *polis*, or of the *demos*, and that is not exhausted or even interestingly informed by questions about his efficacy as a politician. But the primary purpose of the book will be to take seriously the philosophic impulses behind the widespread thought that Mr. Obama is, in the three ways suggested above, post-historical, and to consider the warrant for this impulse and the prospects for plausibly fleshing it out.

Before taking up the questions of Mr. Obama's claim to post-historical status, or of some part or parts of the world's claim to this status in light of Mr. Obama's election, it is important to get clear on what this status involves. Some of this clarity will come from the chapters that follow, as each follows out a particular way of being post-historical. But a couple of issues need to get settled sooner, in order to lay the groundwork for the discussion to come. First I'll need to discuss the general condition of being post-historical, in order to identify the broad framework that will govern the narrower discussions of race, partisanship, and political community. Then I'll need to lay some groundwork for thinking responsibly about race, a topic that will demand our attention even beyond the chapter that is specifically devoted to it. The rest of this introduction will be devoted to those tasks.

The core notions in play in this study—post-racial, post-partisan, and post-imperial—employ the distinctive approach to temporality that philosophers and others now commonly signal with the prefix, "post-." This approach has its roots in historicist thinkers like Hegel and Marx, but has over time become popular in a variety of domains. The prefix now routinely appears as a kind of philosophical operator, as shorthand for an argument—I've suggested elsewhere that we call these "posterizing arguments"[3]—about the proper orientation to history. We see these kinds of arguments now in relation to, among many other things, industrial civilization, urban spaces, soul culture, the civil rights era, analytic philosophy, modern art practices, and, of course, modernity itself.

Posterizing arguments differ in their details, of course, but the basic structure is the same in each case. Something has been repudiated, transcended, or otherwise left behind, and has left in its wake a space for something new. It is not yet clear, and may never be clear, how to think about what is filling the space. But whatever this novelty is, it is rooted in the conditions that it supersedes.

The "post-" functions in these situations as what Kwame Anthony Appiah calls a "space-clearing gesture": as a way of creating distance from some older way of proceeding.[4] But insisting on the "post-"—which is to say, continuing to orient oneself to what came before instead of marking the emergence of novelty with a wholly new vocabulary—indicates both the debt to the past and the difficulty, perhaps impossibility, of capturing this novelty in any existing vocabularies. In this sense, then, posterizing is all at once a gesture of repudiation, of indebtedness, of skepticism, and of openness, all with an eye toward the inexorability of change over time. One might say that the "post-" in "post-racial" and such terms is akin to the "post-" in "posterity," and we know, Freud reminds us, of the often-vexed relationships between parents and children, older generations and newer ones.

With this account of posterizing arguments in hand, we can say that appeals to post-racial, post-partisan, and post-imperial conditions will at the very least involve attempts to clear some space, even if it isn't clear what comes next. The authors of the appeals might be pointing to shifts that have already happened, or they might be trying to hasten along a shift that is only starting to make itself felt. But what will be at stake in every case is the thought that we are at least on the brink of an historic change in course, and that in some sense, to some degree, the future is in our hands.

As common as posterizing arguments are today, arguments about the unreality or declining significance of race are probably even more common. We will soon consider the possibility that the significance of the Obama presidency is importantly tied to its role in making race matter less, or in making it clear that this shift had already taken place. In order to evaluate this possibility properly, it is important to get clear on just what "race" means, or has meant, or used to mean (or whatever), and on the language I'll use to talk about this. What I say about race in what follows will pass lightly over a great many empirical and conceptual details that with more time we might study with profit. It will also draw heavily on ideas that I've worked out in detail elsewhere.[5]

The concept of race emerged more or less in the fifteenth century, in the cultures we would eventually think of as "Western," as an instrument for understanding and acting on human difference. It took quite some time for this project to take the shape that we've come to know in places like the US, but the basic impulse has always been the same: to sort the human population into interesting subgroups by assigning generic meanings to human bodies and bloodlines. The impulse predated the emergence of the concept, and worked itself out in some contexts by appeal to different concepts. I will focus here on the contexts—in modern Europe and in the orbit of European empires—that helped themselves to explicitly racial vocabularies.

Eventually this racialist impulse hardened into the classical racialist conviction that begins to define the sort of race-thinking that most people find familiar now. Classical racialism holds first that the human family consists of a handful of populations, each distinguished by a characteristic set of inheritable traits; second, that these traits include physical, often easily visible, traits like skin color and hair texture, as well as non-physical traits like intelligence and capacity for ethical self-regulation; and third, that these clusters of traits justify ranking the different races on a scale of differential worth. Eventually these rankings were thought by many to have the backing of state of the art scientific inquiry.

Classical racialism was not just an epistemological project, aimed at understanding human difference; it was also a political project, aimed at justifying the racial dimensions of modern social hierarchies. Slavery, colonization, sexual abuse, forced or blocked migration, even, in the limit case, extermination: all may be permissible when the labor, lands, bodies, and lives in question belong to inferior human types. In light of the ease with which race-thinking was turned to this use, and in light of the way race-thinking emerged alongside modern conceptions of equality and freedom *and* alongside modern colonial practices, we might describe the original racialist impulse differently. The aim was to sort the human population into interesting subgroups, *and* to do this in a context shaped by the determination to monetize overseas adventures and to reconcile a promising path to monetization with emerging conceptions of ethical conduct. And so we did, creating in the process the familiar, color-coded, continentally based modern races—black, brown, red, white, and yellow.

The race concept became a valuable resource for oppressive and exploitative social arrangements, but it also quickly became a resource for contesting those arrangements. The basic impulse—find interesting human sub-groups—quickly expressed itself in activist and diagnostic approaches to the concept of race. For these critical racialists, the enduring trait that linked the members of these populations needn't be an inheritable physical and non-physical essence. It might instead be the shared and reliable likelihood of being subjected to racist treatment by people and institutions in the grip of classical racialism, or a shared upbringing in the segregated social worlds that classical racialism created.

(These critical racialisms are, incidentally, the approaches that come into play when people resist the charge that Mr. Obama is not really black. It is true that he cannot trace his roots to African-descended people who lived in the US during slavery or Jim Crow segregation. It is also true that he is mixed, with as good a claim on biological grounds, if that makes sense, to whiteness as to blackness, and, thanks to the years he spent growing up in Indonesia, nearly as good a claim on cultural grounds to being Asian. The first thing to say here is that blackness is a racial position and African American identity is an ethnic status. These overlap but are not identical. The second thing to say is that, on the conception of race I've just sketched, one can be mixed *and* black, or black in one context and more saliently something else in another. The third thing to say is what Mr. Obama himself has said: he has consciously embraced a black American identity, which is not dispositive but is significant; and even if he hadn't embraced it, the world would likely orient itself to his body in ways that would quickly urge him to think of himself as black, just to make sense of his experiences.)

This quick and dirty genealogy of the race concept should make three things clear. First, "race" is a fluid and dynamic concept, working differently, getting invented, applied, and reinvented differently, in different contexts. Second, it is irreducibly contingent and political, an artifact of human social practices and power relations. And third, the probity of the concept—the reality of whatever it is the concept means to denote—depends on the uses to which it is put. Classical racialism appears to be indefensible, just based on what we know about human biological variation. But this tells us nothing yet about more critical modes of race-thinking, whether these emerge from political struggles against racism or, say, from scientific inquiries into the utility of superficial racial distinctions—skin color, ancestral homeland, and so on—for the purposes of medical diagnosis and treatment.

The Obama presidency is not only a racial phenomenon, of course, not least because nothing is. Race is just one axis of social differentiation, one dimension along which we live out our multidimensional lives. As multiple generations of black feminists and others have shown, no one navigates the world just as a member of a race. We are much more than this, though race can surely matter to the way we live in these other dimensions.[6]

Similarly, neither the presidency nor the person of Barack Obama can be understood simply as a racial phenomenon. Race surely matters to both, even if it matters, as we'll soon see people claiming, mainly by showing us that we need to stop acting as if race matters. But they are about much more than race. I will argue in what follows that the importance of these things, of this man and of the political institutions that he embodies and inhabits, have importantly to do with the prospect of historical transcendence. During his first campaign, Mr. Obama—I will refer to him in this way, as "Mr. Obama" or "President Obama" rather than simply, in typical academic fashion, by reference to his last name, in order to distinguish him from the other occupants of the White House, and of the institution of the presidency, who share this last name— invited people to think of him as the harbinger or emissary of change, if not quite as its heroic agent. The burden of this book will be to consider just what it means to take a version of this thought seriously.

NOTES

1 Barack Obama, "Remarks by the President at the 50th Anniversary of the Selma to Montgomery Marches," March 7, 2015, accessed March 20, 2015 at https:// www.whitehouse.gov/the-press-office/2015/03/07/remarks-president-50th-anniversary-selma-montgomery-marches

2 William James, *Some Problems of Philosophy*, in *Writings, 1902–1910* (1911; New York: Library of America, 1987) 1057.

3 "Post-Black, Old Black," *African American Review* 41:4 – Special Issue on Post-Soul Aesthetics (2007), 625–640.

4 Kwame Anthony Appiah, *In My Father's House* (New York: Oxford University Press, 1992) 149.

5 Paul C. Taylor, *Race: A Philosophical Introduction* (Cambridge, UK: Polity—Blackwell, 2004; 2nd ed. 2013).

6 For a canonical statement of this view, *see* Kimberlé Crenshaw, *"Demarginalizing the Intersection of Race and Sex: A Black Feminist Critique of Antidiscrimination Doctrine, Feminist Theory and Antiracist Politics,"* University of Chicago Legal Forum 1989: 139–167.

One

INTRODUCTION

During the run-up to Barack Obama's election in 2008, and shortly afterwards, it was hard to avoid references to post-racialism in mainstream political discourse. If Farai Chideya is right, only references to hope and change were easier to come by.[1] Fascination with the idea spanned the range of respectable political opinion. From James Taranto's column in the *Wall Street Journal* on the right to David Remnick's *New Yorker* essay on the liberal semi-left, everyone seemed ready to consider the possibility that Mr. Obama was the culmination or repudiation of the history of US racial politics—or at the very least, as one of Mr. Remnick's interviewees put it, that the new president represented a break in the rhythm of that history.[2]

Looking back now, it is much harder to find anyone willing to credit the idea that the US had somehow transcended race-thinking in 2008. To be fair, there was some diffidence about the idea even then. Balancing the eager and breezy embrace of the idea in places like the *New York Daily News*[3] was a somewhat less common but still substantial current of more sober reflections in places like *TheGrio.com*. Remnick, for example, repeatedly asks his subjects whether Obama's election signals the arrival of a post-racial era, and they repeatedly tell him that it doesn't. And in the early days of the 2012 campaign season, Obama himself declared in an interview with *Rolling Stone* that he had never bought the post-racial line at all.[4]

The "Obama as post-racial herald" meme, as dubiously sourced and ambivalently advanced as it has been, might seem to have only a meager claim—at best—on anyone's philosophical attention. These armchair exercises in the philosophy of racial history nevertheless interest me, for at least three reasons. First, some of the appeals to post-racialism are not at all ambivalent, and come not from news column filler pieces like Taranto's or even from long-form, thoughtful journalistic essays like Remnick's, but from scholars engaged more or less diligently in close argumentation. These people believe that we *have* become post-racial, and that Mr. Obama's election either reveals or underwrites that fact, or does both, more clearly than any other event. They believe furthermore that saying this is important for reasons more related to getting things right than to providing timely content for a newspaper or website. Serious reflection like this deserves serious consideration.

A second reason to consider the idea of Obama as post-racial herald is that expressions of this idea represent the most obvious and most common ways to insist on the president's post-historical status. This insistence is, as I've already noted, somewhat uneven and ambivalent. But this fact in my view just adds to its philosophical interest, not least because it involves ambivalence in something like the clinical sense. It is a matter not just of hesitation in the face of an idea or, as I said above, diffidence, but of closely matched forces working in opposition to each other, marking some object of attention as *simultaneously* attractive *and* repellent. Or: Remnick's essay repudiates the idea of post-racialism, but does this so insistently that one gets the feeling that he protests too much—especially since his argument dovetails neatly with his depiction of Obama, in the book that his essay anticipated, as "the bridge" between regimes of racial politics. It is, in other words, worth asking: What is it about this idea that draws people to it even as it announces itself to most of those same people as unambiguously false?

A third and final reason to consider the prospect of Obama's post-racial heraldry here is that one might defensibly define philosophy as the attempt to comprehend one's age in thought. Put differently, and translating from Hegel to Dewey, one might say that philosophy is criticism—criticism of the influential beliefs that underlie and underwrite the current state of a culture. If that's right, then it is surely philosophically worthwhile to consider the fact that significant numbers of people were for a time attracted, however briefly or unevenly, to an image of Obama as the herald of post-racialism.

In light of all this, I will devote this chapter to the prospect of post-raciality in Mr. Obama's America. I want to consider just what "post-racialism" means, what racial history has to be in order for appeals to post-racialism to make sense, whether the US has in fact become post-racial in any of the relevant senses of the term, and why people who doubt that we are post-racial might still be drawn to the idea.

FOUR APPROACHES TO POST-RACIALISM

The claim that US society has become post-racial can be understood in a variety of different ways. Some of these will turn out to make rather little contact with the real world, with its persistent inequalities, hierarchies, and prejudices. But it would be a mistake to dismiss the idea altogether because of the inadequacies of its more simplistic articulations. The more complex formulations of the idea deserve more sustained attention than they have sometimes received. And the prominence of the idea, its persistence in our discursive environments, deserves some effort at diagnosis as well.

At least four different approaches to post-racialism can be distilled from the ferment surrounding Mr. Obama's first presidential run. It turns out that more complicated and interesting approaches emerge from careful consideration of the limits of the simpler, more objectionable ones. So I will on occasion in what follows refer to these as "grades" or "levels" of post-racialist discourse.

The first, simplest grade of post-racialism reduces to post-*racism*—to the thought that racism has been defeated, transcended, or otherwise put in history's rear-view mirror. The second grade denies that racism is dead, but insists that the arc of history is bending toward anti-racism. The third form of post-racialism denies that history is a seamless upward march away from racism, but it insists on the attractiveness of a post-racialist ethical vision and on the importance of keeping the vision before us. Finally, the fourth form accepts that it is a gamble to insist on the post-racialist's ethical vision: It grants the possibility that there may be some danger in prematurely opposing racialism to a cosmopolitan or universalist vision of human sodality. But it insists that the gamble is worth taking, the experiment is worth running, and that avoiding the risk will necessarily and tragically mean forgoing the possible gains for human fellowship and social justice.

These four approaches to post-racialism came into view during the debates that occurred in the wake of Mr. Obama's election. In contributions to traditional and social media, to popular conversations and scholarly exchanges, people all over the world considered whether the 2008 election was a decisive turning point in the battle against invidious or vicious racial distinctions and practices. Mr. Obama's campaign, election, and public persona served each of these approaches well, though in different ways. And, perhaps surprisingly, each approach has something to recommend it. That is to say, each one gets something right, and gets something *importantly* right. Unfortunately, each on balance obscures more than it illuminates, about Mr. Obama and about the moment he seemed to usher in.

POST-RACIALISM 1: AFTER RACISM

The first grade of post-racialist discourse has the virtue of being straightforward and clear. Unfortunately for its adherents, it seems not to have any other virtues. We find our way to this version of post-racialism when some watershed event—the election of a president, the confirmation of a Supreme Court justice, the hiring of a high-profile CEO—happens to involve someone who happens not to be a white man. The event would not of course have been possible in the bad old days of racial injustices like Chinese Exclusion Acts and Jim Crow segregation. So the occurrence of the event seems to this sort of post-racialist to show that we've consigned racism and race-based injustice to the dustbin of history. And since, on this view, there's no reason to talk about race except in furtherance of some unethical conduct or vicious attitude, the watershed event reveals that race-thinking itself is obsolete. All of which is supposed to demonstrate, as one *Wall Street Journal* article put it, "the pointlessness of dwelling on race" (Taranto, par. 7).

The argument of course goes by much too quickly, and provokes some obvious objections. *Racism still exists*, the objections begin. *True enough, we now frown on explicit acts of discrimination and open avowals of racial animus. But there's quite good psychological evidence that we still harbor implicit biases that belie our conscious affirmations and shape our immediate responses to each other. What's more, even if racism were no more, it shaped society deeply enough when it was around to leave us all sorts of racial "gaps"— the achievement gap, the wealth gap, and so on—that we still have to contend with.*

All of which is a way of specifying precisely what the crudeness of this first, crude form of post-racialism consists in. The view seems essentially to be that we have gotten beyond racism, and that racism is nothing but a matter of individual, conscious expressions of race-based ill-will or prejudice. The weight of scholarly opinion in sociology, psychology, political science, philosophy, legal studies, and all the other fields that take racism seriously is that this is precisely not the way to think of racism, whichever of the many alternatives one chooses. One might appeal to subconscious biases that belie our express egalitarian commitments, or to vicious attitudes that undermine our express commitments, or to institutional structures that reproduce racial disadvantage without the mediation of any conscious racial intent, or to ideological and ideational structures that frame our conceptions of our fellows and of our relationships to them. Or, perhaps most plausibly, we might think of the idea of racism as a perennially, perhaps essentially, contested concept, or as a free-floating vehicle for expressing disapproval of bad conduct in racialized situations. On this reading there is no single best account of racism, because we use the term in different ways in different settings, to achieve different purposes.

Whichever of these more complicated approaches to racism one chooses, one will be hard-pressed to endorse the quick dismissal of racism that characterizes the crude form of post-racialism. Whether one thinks racism is most saliently a matter of institutional structures or of implicit biases—or, as is most likely, of both, intertwined—the *Wall Street Journal* writer's triumphalism is unwarranted and ill advised. Many advocates of post-racial discourse recognize this, and move swiftly to distance themselves from this crude, post-racist version of the view.

POST-RACIALISM 2: FROM A *FAIT ACCOMPLI* TO AN UNFOLDING FUTURE

In a widely circulated piece from *theGrio.com*, linguist and commentator John McWhorter (2010) refuses the seductions of crude post-racialism while drawing out the intuition that gives the view whatever attractiveness it has. The impulse to put race behind us is a reflection of the sense that something, something important, has changed when it comes to race. The change needn't involve the complete abolition or transcendence of racism—which, McWhorter notes, we have not achieved—in order to count as a real change. So knee-jerk skepticism about post-racialism, he suggests, is really a roundabout invitation to affirm the lasting salience of racism, and one can reasonably accept this invitation while still insisting on the reality and importance of the things that have changed. One might even think of the language of post-racialism as a way of insisting on these changes, and of highlighting their depth and magnitude.

Bakari Kitwana echoes and deepens McWhorter's claim that a richer, more complicated sense of post-racialism can capture something that escapes our knee-jerk embraces and aversions. Despite the fact that "those on the far left almost instantly find [the idea] offensive and those on the right are almost too eager to embrace it," this "new concept has emerged" because "[t]here is something that Americans in this moment, in this time, are . . . feeling that we've never felt before."[5] What is this feeling?

> [W]hat we arrive at in the word "post-racial" is a sentiment that speaks to the cognitive dissonance between the reality and the illusion of race. This feeling certainly demands a word. The one that we've settled on for now evolved out of previous eras and still carries their baggage. All of those using

it accept that something has changed, even if they can't agree on what it is. "Post-racial," for lack of a better word, is attempting to speak to this new idea.[6]

Historian David Hollinger clarifies the sense of dissonance that, in Kitwana's view, motivates the (non-non-starter) appeals to post-racialism. In an extension of his famous early reflections on post-ethnicity (Hollinger 1995, 2011), Hollinger points out that many serious and thoughtful people have appealed to notions like "post-raciality" and "post-ethnicity" in recent years, and have done so without daring to deny that "racism continues to be a problem . . . in the United States" (2011, p. 175). After pointing out that "a discursive Grand Canyon" yawns between the claims of serious post-racialists claim and what (we can now call) post-racists, Hollinger goes on to explain more carefully what the claim actually involves for him (2011, p. 174). His explanation goes something like this: Race of course has mattered historically and still matters. But the ways in which it matters have changed and continue to change. These changes have in general to do with a kind of decreased "intensity," which registers for us—if we're paying attention—in the form of at least these three realizations: that our social affiliations—including our ethnoracial affiliations—are not natural and fixed but contingent and can be chosen, *or not*; that ethnoracial politics and affiliations are not obviously the best resources for addressing social ills; and that our main ethnoracial categories have never been and cannot be as pure and inviolate as we once pretended they were.

As Hollinger sees it, now that we take seriously the gap—the dissonance, Kitwana would say—between the way race-talk invites us to imagine our identities and affiliations and the way those things actually work in the real world, we have begun to take seriously the various inadequacies from which ethnoracial vocabularies suffer. Three areas of inadequacy stand out for the careful post-racialist: social-theoretic, ethical, and political.

First, scrutinizing social problems and phenomena through racial lenses tends to obscure more than it reveals, not least because race doesn't work the way we once thought it did. For people thinking about social life in the wake of nineteenth and early twentieth century ideas about human difference, racial boundaries seemed fixed and clear, and seemed clearly to mark the distribution of important human traits like intelligence, temperance, and moral worth. Physical science now tells us that human traits aren't distributed like that, and history tells us that human populations have never been hermetically sealed off from each other. If we want to understand why different populations fare differently in society, and what human biological diversity really means, appealing to racial traits will do us little good.

Just as we have come to see the shortcomings of ethnoracial practices when employed as instruments of social theory, we have also become aware of the ethical limits of these practices. We usually think that everyone has a racial identity, and this strikes us as important information. If we don't know how to classify someone then we are eager to figure it out. And if someone refuses to play along with the game of racial classification, either by assigning themselves a surprising identity or by refusing classification altogether, we often think of them as deluded or confused. This prescriptive and obligatory dimension of racial identity puts it in tension with key ethical norms relating to individuality and freedom. That is to say: we should be free to associate ourselves, or not, with whatever we choose. For broadly existential and perhaps aesthetic purposes, some people still choose to identify themselves as members of ethnoracial groups. But more of us than ever before are making this choice a voluntaristic and, in a way, playful spirit, self-consciously free from any social requirement to do so, and freed from the burdens of boundary-policing.

Finally, race also fares poorly as an instrument of political mobilization. Political movements and organizations built on racial foundations tend to have at least three broad difficulties. They overlook or refuse potentially useful inter-racial affiliations across racial boundaries. They overlook or deny intra-racial issues, thereby subordinating the interests of some members of the race to the interests of others. And they promise more in the way of solidarity and stability than they earn, as the natural ties of race are sometimes assumed to obviate the need for the hard work of mobilizing and organizing.

For all of these reasons, the careful post-racialist can argue that we are better off in turning away from talk of races and ethnicities and toward other analytical and ethical frameworks—*even in our attempts to deal with (what we a bit misleadingly call) racial injustice*. This move needn't involve the dismissive, grandly optimistic gestures that we saw in the *Wall Street Journal*. It begins with a point that most of us already accept—that race-talk is ethically and empirically problematic—and move from there to the recognition that people in at least some places have come to organize their affairs and understand themselves in ways that allow them, that allow us, to make our suspicion of race-talk operative in our lives. This is why Hollinger can distance his version of post-racialism from the stronger claims that await on the other side of his discursive Grand Canyon. His point, a point he shares with McWhorter, Kitwana, and others, is not that the problems we attribute to race are illusory, either because they have been solved or were never all that important. Nor is the point that beliefs about race have no bearing on social life, or that racial meanings can play no role in the organization of post-racial communities and the formation of post-racial selves. The point is just that race-thinking has, to a significant degree and for good reasons, *lost its hold* on us, that this is a salutary development, and that we should signal this shift in our language.

Unfortunately, the careful post-racialist's key claim, the one that distinguishes his or her view from the crude, *WSJ* variety, is where the trouble begins. The claim is that race still matters but *not as much* as it once did (and, obviously, as everyone on all sides agrees, not in the same ways as it once did). We might think of this as a way of doubling down on William Julius Wilson's famous claim—which he has since repudiated—about the declining significance of race.[7] On this approach, race has receded far enough from the centers of our private and public lives to require a change in our practices of expression, our policy choices, and our habits of imagination. Proceeding in any other way would leave us out of phase with the historical moment we inhabit.

But this use of the declining significance claim runs together two points that are very different in meaning and in plausibility.

It is one thing to say that race has changed. It is another thing entirely to render this change as something like a linear, downward-sloping trendline. To change is not yet, and not necessarily, to decline, both in general and in the particular case of racial practices. As Hollinger's colleague Waldo Martin (2011) points out, racial practices have changed, to be sure, as have the contexts in which we participate in them, but they have both declined *and persisted.* Their importance—or what Hollinger calls their "intensity"—may have decreased in some ways, but it has manifestly increased in others.

Distinguishing change from decline shows that this second grade of post-racial discourse is still too quick, its careful repudiation of crude post-racism notwithstanding. We can see this more clearly turning back to the case of President Obama. His campaign successes have been taken as markers of racial progress, since one could hardly have imagined a black man ascending to the presidency just a few years back. But this achievement was precisely *not* a matter of people overcoming racial attitudes and voting their hopes while somehow purified of bias. Rather, as Tesler and Sears argue on the basis of extensive survey data, "racial attitudes [were among] the most important determinants of how the American public responded to [President Obama]."[8] They explain:

> [R]acial attitudes were heavily implicated in every aspect of Barack Obama's quest for the White House. From Americans' earliest evaluations of candidate Obama to their primary voting to their general election vote choice, Obama was heavily judged in terms of his racial background. Racial attitudes were strongly associated with both support for and opposition to Obama throughout the election year. With these positive and negative effects largely canceling themselves out in Obama's aggregate vote tallies, many mistakenly took his victory as a sign that race no longer mattered in American politics. Behind such success in the primaries and general election, however, lay perhaps the most racialized presidential voting patterns in American history.[9]

In deference to facts like these, Martin refuses Hollinger's post-racialism by invoking Amiri Baraka's idea of the "changing same."[10] Baraka used this expression to insist on the continuities in black expressive culture that made it possible to link early forms like the blues to later ones like R&B, formal and stylistic differences notwithstanding. Martin emulates this move in the domain of politics, which enables him to say things like this: "I see more fundamental continuity than real change in the status of African Americans in the late twentieth and early twenty-first centuries."[11] That is: we could never have plausibly imagined a black president before, so Obama's election does represent a real shift. But that shift has little to do with a decline in significance or decrease in the intensity of race-thinking. It's not that race matters less, but that it matters differently.

Beyond reading the empirical tea leaves of Obama's electoral successes, there are a variety of ways to demonstrate the continuity-across-change in US racial politics. We might appeal to statistics about the race gaps that I mentioned above, or complicate the simple narratives of linear ethical progress—from unfreedom to freedom, in a ceaseless upward march toward actualizing the Constitution's better moments—that often inform popular readings of racial history. Then again, we might join Michele Alexander and the other, more radical thinkers who preceded her down this path, in linking our contemporary approaches to policing and prisons to older methods of racialized social control stretching back to the beginning of the Jim Crow era.[12]

Assuming the availability and probity of stories like these, I'll refrain from rehearsing the facts and turn instead to the philosophical work of providing a wider frame for the facts. Careful post-racialism is right to insist that there has been a shift in our racial practices, and to insist that the shift is too important to dismiss with a casual gesture at the persistence of racism. It is, however, wrong to read this shift as a seamless turn away from confusion and toward enlightenment. It is better thought of as a shift, or constellation of shifts, in the relationships between, and the contents of, the two dominant *racial institutional orders* in the US.

King and Smith developed the idea of racial orders in an attempt to capture both the centrality of race to American politics and the centrality of institutional orders to racial politics.[13] On their account, institutional orders are "coalitions of state institutions and other political actors and organizations that seek to secure and exercise governing power. . . ."[14] *Racial* institutional orders are orders in which race is central: "ones in which political actors have adopted (and often adapted) racial concepts, commitments, and aims in order to help bind together their coalitions and structure governing institutions. . . ."[15] Two such orders have dominated and shaped US history and politics: one committed in various ways over time to anti-racist egalitarian transformation, and the other committed, in various ways over time, to white supremacy or other "anti-transformative" orientations.[16] These orders are intertwined and coevolving, changing shape and content not in lockstep but in dialectical relationship.

King and Smith explain what it means for racial institutional orders to evolve:

> [O]ne predominant order gives way to another, or . . . the prevailing order's leading concepts of racial goals, rules, roles, and boundaries are substantially revised, as when most white supremacists felt compelled to abandon slavery or when most racial egalitarians came to insist on equal voting rights, not just civil rights. Such development can arise from struggles among . . . groups within an institutional order, from the interactions of racial orders with other orders, such as labor and party systems, and from broad social . . . changes, all of which may strengthen some participants in an order and weaken others, or add new players and policy challenges for the order to confront.[17]

The appeal to institutional orders gives us a way to credit what careful post-racialism gets right while avoiding its overstatements. What the view properly registers is the shift, one might say, from a post-segregation racial order to a post-civil rights order. Reading this as a shift in racial orders makes clear what even careful post-racialism threatens to miss or obscure: that, as Martin says, our racial practices have both declined and persisted.

The case for treating the (ostensibly) post-racial shift as a seamless journey away from race-thinking is straightforward. The breakthroughs of the civil rights era effectively brought *de jure* segregation to an end, and did so just as skepticism about racial categories started to take root among influential knowledge producers. Anti-racist egalitarianism has become the ethical common sense for most people, and the transformative order that made this possible moved from the margins of our politics to the center. We can see this re-centering in Thurgood Marshall's journey from crusading oppositional lawyer to Supreme Court justice, and in the many other stories like his. But we can also see it in the ready embrace of anti-racist principles by political figures with clear ties to the old white supremacist order, like former Chief Justice William Rehnquist and his many protégés.

Unfortunately for the post-racialist, the case for the continued significance of race despite this shift is similarly straightforward. Despite the wide currency of post-segregation, egalitarian principles, many people and political forces "remained protective of arrangements that the Jim Crow system had generated, especially ... the overrepresentation of whites at the top of most ... institutions."[18] As a result, an antitransformative racial order has inherited the role of the older, explicitly white supremacist orders, which are now ethically beyond the pale for most people. The key feature of this order is its determination to use facially race-neutral principles and arguments to oppose measures aimed at reducing racial inequality. To be clear: the claim here is not that the anti-transformative order is constituted by closet racists who cynically dupe themselves or others into thinking that they are committed to anti-racist principles that they in fact oppose. The claim is that for a variety of reasons and in a variety of contexts, too many of each to detail here, even race-neutral and anti-racist arguments have racial implications, and some of these mirror the outcomes that white supremacist racial orders sought to bring about. Some of these reasons are related to the affective establishment of racial privilege as an evaluative baseline and of challenges to that privilege as something like theft,[19] while others are in fact related to the cynical manipulation of implicit racial attitudes for political advantage. But it is not necessary to locate the precise balance of reasons in play to make the overall point: Yes, things have changed with regard to race; but the changes are too complicated to read as simple affirmations of the declining significance of race.

That is: It is now possible for a black man to become the president of the United States. But it is also possible for black people to suffer disproportionate levels of surveillance and violence at the hands of the police, and to have the justice system handle their cases and the cases of similarly situated white people differently. Which means that the idea of post-racialism must reckon with the spectacle of the first black president asking for calm when US judicial systems seemed to affirm that black lives in Ferguson, Missouri and Sanford, Florida had no value.

POST-RACIALISM 3: FROM PREDICTION TO PROPHECY

The serious post-racialist can grant the damage done to the argument by the racial orders/changing same critique, and by the cruel juxtaposition of Barack Obama and Trayvon Martin, while still insisting on a deeper and more interesting point. Hollinger's argument in some places has as much to do with envisioning a future as with reading the present, and more to do with imagining a future than with predicting one. So an even more careful post-racialism comes into view once we shift from the thought that race is declining in significance and will continue to do so to the thought that it *should* decline in significance, and that we can help realize this imperative by imagining the post-racial future even now.

Words like "post-racial," Hollinger contends, point to a future in which ethnoracial categories have lost their hold on our identities, our politics, and our quest for economic justice. "No one," he points out, "calls into question the desirability of such a future" (2011, p. 175). But when invited to reflect on this possible future under the rubric of post-racialism, academics and journalists want "to talk only about whether that future has arrived" (2011, p. 175). They overlook the degree to which references to post-raciality are aids to reflection and resources for moral imagination. This new racial vocabulary can help us "sharpen our vision of what a society long accustomed to . . . ascribing and enforcing ethnoracial distinctions might look like if those abhorrent protocols could be weakened" (2011, p. 174). The language of post-racialism, on this approach, is about helping to bring the post-racial future into being, not about shackling our moral imaginations to readings of present conditions or to projections based on them.

To make post-racialism prescriptive and visionary rather than descriptive and extrapolative is, in a sense, to make it a prophecy rather than a prediction. I am using a notion of prophecy something like the one that attaches to practices of religious social criticism. Cornel West explains that in this sense, prophecy insists on "the capacity of human beings to transform their circumstances, engage in relentless criticism and self-criticism, and project visions, analyses, and practices of social freedom."[20] The prophetic commitments to transformation, criticism, and the projection of an ethical vision shine through in some moments of Hollinger's account of post-racialism, and make sense of the view's continued appeal to people who accept the richer account of the racialized social landscape that the racial orders approach offers us.

Considering the case of President Obama helps show the appeal of a prophetic turn for the post-racialist. What made the 2008 election interesting, one might argue, was not the evidence it provided for claims about the US having already transcended race. Anyone who was paying attention would have known that Obama was, as one writer put it, a bound man,[21] boxed in by racial prejudices and expectations on all sides; and that this fact, alongside the kinds of considerations that emerge from a racial orders or (as we'll soon say) racial formation approach to these issues, fairly entailed that Obama's election would not save us from wrestling with racial issues. What actually made the election interesting, this thought continues, was its relocation of the horizon of the possible, and its remapping of the plausible scope for moral imagination and ethical vision. To take a simple example: A black man in the White House enables black parents to rehearse for their children with more confidence than they ever could before that common expression of parental encouragement: *you can be anything you want to be.* Obama is a perfect fit for this post-racial moment in part because he embodies the revelations and possibilities that have begun to weaken our attachment to the "abhorrent protocols" of racial identification, affiliation, and analysis. A black man with a white mother, an Asian sister, loyal voters of all races, no blood ties to slavery, and no political ties to the civil rights enterprise—what better emblem could we have of the prospects for a world beyond race?

This prophetic turn might block the worry that, in different forms, undermines the first two grades of post-racialist discourse. So far the worry has been that the view just gets the world wrong, whether it pretends that racism is no more or that race-thinking is simply on the decline. But by raising the question of the uses and effects of language, it points in the direction of another difficulty. By insisting on the ethical functions of certain kinds of expressive choices, on the role that linguistic resources play in helping us imagine alternate futures and project visions for moral improvement, Hollinger moves the debate into range of a worry rooted precisely in concerns about the ethical functions of the language.

This new worry, ably articulated by Bonilla-Silva and Dietrich (2011), holds that the main problem for post-racialism has less to do with the accuracy of its world-pictures than with the political uses to which its claims get put.[22] These uses become available because the language of post-racialism is neatly suited to blurring the distinction between more and less crude ways of describing the post-civil rights condition. As a result, even the serious and visionary formulations of post-racialism can feed into the unserious and reactionary arguments that use talk of colorblindness—which Hollinger, to his credit, explicitly rejects—to advance a distinctive, late-white-supremacist racial project.

To speak of racial projects in this way is to explore a thought that is adjacent to, and related to, the appeal to racial orders from the previous section. The idea of a racial project (in the form I use— there are others) comes from the racial formation theory of sociologists Michael Omi and Howard Winant, who argue that racial discourse is just one side of the complex social process by which racial categories take shape and do their work. The other side of the process involves the material redistributions that shifts in racial vocabularies help to motivate, justify, and explain. And these two sides evolve together in historical phases that we can think of as racial projects, and that give content to particular regimes of racial politics. On this approach, the idea that we have achieved a post-racial condition is the ideological content of a particular racial paradigm. What distinguishes this paradigm is not its transcendence of race or its prophetic envisioning of a world without race, but its determination to "whitewash" racial history and the mechanisms of ongoing racial stratification—to obscure, ignore, or erase the evidence that race still matters in a variety of definite, concrete, and distressingly familiar ways. Appeals to colorblindness figure prominently in this paradigm, as they invoke what they depict as the ethical common sense of the post-civil rights era to block any reference to racial inequalities or hierarchies.

The key to a racial formation reading of prophetic post-racialism is recognizing that the very act of articulating the post-racial prophecy does the work of an explicitly racial—that is, non-post-racial—politics. For committed adherents to the ideology of colorblindness, real racial justice often enough means refusing race-thinking altogether. On this view, race-based affirmative action programs, anti-racist expressions of racial solidarity, and race-sensitive data-gathering, undertaken to track our progress toward material equality across racial boundaries, should all go the way of the black codes, racially restrictive covenants, and anti-miscegenation laws. Perhaps most important, becoming colorblind in this sense means losing interest in the long, sordid history of what we once called "race relations." This history provides the context for contemporary debates about everything from segregated schools to the corrections industry, but it can of course have no bearing on a world in which *nous avons changé tout cela*. For the most vocal advocates of colorblindness, *history* has no color, which means that the role of color distinctions *in* history, in driving the historical processes that created the world we now inhabit, has no bearing on the conduct of our lives. And this brings us back to a version of crude post-racialism.

The prophetic post-racialist might explicitly disavow the slide into crude colorblindness, but this does not get to the heart of the racial formation worry. Shifting our focus from individual assertions to discursively loaded racial projects makes the disavowal pointless, and reminds us that the issue now is the ideational work, the framing or agenda-setting, that comes with appeals to color-blindness. One way to put the point is to say that the plausibility of the prophetic view, with its hope that we can imagine the end of race, and almost see it from here, trickles down to cruder arguments about where things stand now.

To see how this "trickle-down" process of unearned discursive plausibility works, we can draw from Stephen Steinberg's account of semantic infiltration.[23] As Steinberg points out, the work of politics sometimes involves "the appropriation of the language of one's political opponents for the purpose of blurring distinctions and molding [the language] to one's own political position" (116). Daniel Patrick Moynihan's infamous *The Negro Family* report of 1965, like the speech that he co-wrote (with Richard Goodwin) for Lyndon Johnson to deliver in the same year at Howard University, shows how this works. Both texts appropriate and then subvert an influential line of thinking from the left-liberal, or further left, wings of the civil rights movement. They endorse the thought that equal opportunity is not enough, that civil rights triumphs mean little without some structural change. But where civil rights advocates took "structural change" to refer to political economy, to the wider social and economic structures that condition and constrain the pursuit of equality, Moynihan set aside political economy and focused centrally on changes in the *family* structures of different races. And this move launched American political discourse into a generation of arguments about the culture of poverty, "illegitimate" children, and single mothers, by way of language borrowed from arguments about urban policy and the limits of capitalism. (The arguments were of course older than this, but owed their form and currency in this moment to Moynihan's intervention.)

Colorblind ideology works in much the same way as Moynihan's diversion of concrete equality discourse into racial liberalism. It invites us to endorse the anti-racialist thoughts that Hollinger wants us to think—viz., that solidarity must be won, that identities must be chosen, and that neither of these can be assumed on the basis of appearance or ancestry. But it then invites us to reject the other, in some ways more challenging, *anti-racist* thoughts that Hollinger endorses. Where Hollinger-style post-racialism goes on to insist that racism and racial hierarchies have not vanished and that concerns about racial justice should inspire a wider interest in social and economic justice, *colorblind* post-racialism suggests—*using appeals to ideas like "post-racialism"*—that racial hierarchies have vanished along with the presumptive validity of racial solidarities and identities, and that whatever inequalities remain are a function of individuals failing to take advantage of the opportunities now open to them—as it might be, because of the tangle of cultural pathologies that Moynihan saw at the root of "Negro" inequality, and that he thereby helped make part of the content of liberal anti-racism.

We see the trajectory of post-racialist semantic infiltration limned by a striking, in some circles infamous, line from Chief Justice John Roberts' decision in the *Parents Involved v. Seattle* decision. Writing for the court, on the way to striking down desegregation schemes that the cities of Seattle and Louisville had voluntarily adopted, Roberts summarily explains that "[t]he way to stop discrimination on the basis of race is to stop discriminating on the basis of race."[24] This sounds very nice and, at first blush, on some level obviously right. But worries arise on a careful reading of the passage. From the beginning—"The way to stop discrimination on the basis of race"—the passage exudes misplaced confidence, as if non-discrimination, is after all, *of course* what we all want, and as if this goal is obviously either identical to or more important than what some of us call "racial justice," *and* as if there is just one, simple way to achieve this goal. This move peremptorily closes the conceptual space that some people see yawning open—a space between, on the one hand, present, overt, and conscious expressions of individual bias, and, on the other, the routine, impersonal, race-related maldistribution of the benefits and burdens of social cooperation.

Roberts continues: the way to get to the racial promised land "is to stop discriminating on the basis of race," which is to say, to *stop* doing what Louisville and Seattle were doing. Once again we find an important conceptual space closing, this time taking with it the possibility that establishing "whites only" water fountains is not the same thing as using race-thinking to break down the persistent or re-emerging patterns of segregation that the *Brown* decision was supposed to have abolished. The idea is supposed to be that commonsense ethical discourse in the US, burned into our collective psyches by Martin King and others, proscribes *all* race-thinking. This is meant to be an absolute prohibition, applicable whether we use racial categories—which use, on this approach, just is discrimination—for good or for ill. In *Parents Involved* and in the line of cases leading up to it, we find "the question of racial equality [reduced] to mere formalism, completely abstracted from history" or context (Crenshaw 1997, p. 285).

Chief Justice Roberts' sound byte-ready formulation links our post-racial future to "a general rule that nobody's skin color should be taken into account in governmental decision-making" (Crenshaw 1997, p. 284). This means that demonstrable patterns and *recorded histories* of discrimination and exclusion become irrelevant to the distorted and racialized opportunity structures that define contemporary US social life, as do the different purposes to which racial distinctions might be put in public policy. Discrimination is the thing, it turns out, whether the racial classifications in question "seek, not to keep the races apart, but to bring them together."[25] Putting discrimination behind us, in the absolutist, context-independent manner of *Parents Involved*, is the key to the colorblind racial project, and to the over-simple, ideological post-racial sensibility that informs it and is informed by it.

To be clear: Roberts' ultimate conclusion—that race-thinking in public policy is always wrong—might be correct. At the very least, it is not obviously wrong, and nothing I've said so far pre-supposes that it is. The problem is that the argument from colorblindness gets us nowhere near to that conclusion. The usual background assumption, sometimes foregrounded, is that the mere use of racial classifications reinforces the divisions that racial justice must strive to surmount. But the literature on the psychology of prejudice shows that declining to highlight racial distinctions does not prevent people from acting on racial biases. And even if silence about race were the way to break down racial biases, it is hard to imagine it as the way to repair the damage from generations of concrete and specifiable acts and programs of discrimination, domination, oppression, and exclusion.

The colorblind ethic is not obviously wrong, any more than its alternatives are, because there are many questions to answer before we can confidently draw any conclusions about the overall probity of the view. White supremacy in particular and racism in general have done damage, and left scars on the body politic. But perhaps we are so powerless to redress this damage permissibly that we should stop trying and instead chalk it up to history's sunk costs. The problem with the slide from prophetic post-racialism to colorblindness, which is to say, the problem with appeals to post-racialism in a world dominated by colorblind racial projects and antitransformative racial orders, is that the appeal to post-racialism simply does not invite us to take up these questions. It invites us instead—in the context of the colorblind racial project, rather than in the abstract vacuum in which we are often invited to consider it—to entertain the thought that these considerations *can make no claim on our attention at all.*

POST-RACIALISM 4: FROM PROPHECY TO PRAGMATISM

The third approach to post-racialism is the most plausible approach yet, but the move from careful description to prophetic vision serves mostly to reveal the most damaging criticism yet of the post-racialist enterprise. Prophetic post-racialism holds that its ethical vocabulary helps us imagine the better world that we might bring into being, and invites us to focus on the aspects of this world that are already trending in the right direction. In response, critics like Bonilla-Silva point out, in effect, that post-racialist discourse is the semantic side of a colorblind racial project, and that this project uses sophisticated forms of the discourse to motivate and justify its racially patterned distributions of social goods. On this account, it is true but relatively uninteresting that post-racialist language empowers reactionary racist forces and underwrites a reboot of white supremacy. This is uninteresting because anti-racism is now our ethical common sense, and explicit racism requires little in the way of nuance to do its work. What *is* interesting about this critique of the colorblind racial project is that it highlights the ways in which elaborate and misleadingly anodyne campaigns to promote ethical amnesia and sociological myopia do the work of what we sometime still call institutional racism. The worry is that even *sincere* appeals to a race-neutral ethic effectively mask the ongoing processes by which society asymmetrically apportions the resources for well-being along racial lines.

There is one move left to the post-racialist, a move that I've not actually seen anyone make but that the structure of the conceptual space makes available. By pairing the focus on prophetic vision with a kind of pragmatic experimentalism, the post-racialist can liberate our projections of the post-racial future from our present limitations, and insist that the future is still in the making. I invoke pragmatism not in the doctrinaire sense that will be at issue in Chapter 2, but in a broader sense. The key here is not any particular theory of knowledge, language, experience, or democracy, or any particular debts—apart from a guest appearance by William James in a moment—to key figures like Dewey, Locke, Addams, or Peirce. The key here is a general voluntarist commitment to the importance of human agency, which is to say, to the role of active experimentation, undertaken in a fallibilist spirit, in making the world of our experience. In this spirit, the post-racialist might urge us to take up the task of *making* the future specifically by refusing the models of the past, including the models recommended by the racial formation theorist's reading of recent and contemporary racial politics. If the present is as worrisome and the future as bleak as the racial formation approach makes them out to be, then, this view holds, perhaps we should redouble our efforts. We should simply work harder to contest the slippage between post-racialist arguments and colorblind ideology.

The experimentalism in play here is akin to William James' famous "will to believe" argument.[26] James points out in that well-known but often ill-read essay that some facts will not come into being unless we actively believe that they can come into being and work to make them do so. How is it, he asks, that a handful of robbers can take over a train despite being vastly outnumbered by the passengers? (If it helps, and isn't too depressing, you can bring the example up to date by thinking of airplane highjackers.) The passengers could overpower the robbers if they would only try, but they don't think they can, and so they don't. Their hesitation is not unreasonable, since none of the passengers knows whether the others will support an attempt to fight back. But this makes James' point. If one person took the gamble, ran the experiment, and launched a counterattack, the others would be more likely to join in. The first person's belief in the possibilities might make all the difference, and might make the desired outcome more likely.

In a similarly experimental spirit, the post-racialist might argue that Bonilla-Silva and the other critics of the colorblind racial project are like the paralyzed passengers on the highjacked train. They are refusing to work toward the production of a state of affairs that they can help bring about—our emancipation from the abhorrent protocols of race, the achievement of ethical universalism —because they have committed themselves in advance to the impossibility of that state of affairs. Their commitment is not unreasonable, given a sober estimate of the conditions and the odds. But once estimates like this are in place it is of course still possible, and not necessarily unreasonable, to bet on poor odds. This is so in part because the payoff for a winning bet would be so enormous, but also in part, and more saliently right now, because working in support of the less likely outcome will improve the odds of winning.

Unfortunately for the post-racialist, it is not obvious that the post-racial experiment has the sort of structure that James requires. James crafted his will to believe strategy specifically for cases in which the need for action was so great and the prospects for gathering conclusive evidence so small that stepping into the void ceases to be ill-advised. The point of the essay is of course to defend the determination to believe propositions about religion and the divine. We can imagine train-robbing cases that are relevantly similar to the case of the religious believer—cases in which you can't *prove* that my belief is misguided, and the benefits of believing are so great that I should just, as they say, step out on faith. But we can also imagine cases that do not fit this model. So the question for the pragmatic post-racialist is whether committing oneself to the post-racial future is sufficiently like committing oneself to the God hypothesis.

It seems to me that the cases are importantly, profoundly dissimilar. In fact, the post-racialism case is what the case of religious belief would be if willing the belief in God actively undermined one's ability to derive whatever benefits are meant to accrue from the act. Post-racialism imagines free and equal persons creating themselves, affiliating, and cooperating without regard for existing racial boundaries and scripts. But the very idea of post-racialism both presupposes and reinforces a racially circumscribed vision of race in US history. And the social practices and public policies that we build on this vision in turn reinforce the racial gaps and divisions that post-racialism aims to transcend. Or so, in any case, one might argue, without fear of refutation by standard forms of post-racialist argument, which either ignore these dangers in the manner of crude colorblindness or simply roll the dice on the post-racial prophecy despite the dangers.

OBAMA'S POST-RACIALISM

My main aim so far has been to reconsider the thought that Barack Obama's ascension and election constitute the rock on which racial history has been broken. I wanted to see whether reformulating this thought to address certain major criticisms gives it more of a claim on our attention than it generally enjoys. My sense is that even the strongest form of post-racialism is self-undermining, despite its valuable insistence on certain key shifts in our racial practices, and that even the plausible appeals to post-racialism are politically, ethically, and epistemically dangerous, because of the way these appeals articulate with racial projects and racial orders that diminish our chances for productive engagement with the ongoing realities of race-related disadvantage.

With that work out of the way, I'll start to bring this chapter to a close by reflecting on Mr. Obama's own relationship to the idea of post-racialism. He famously, and repeatedly, refused to invoke the idea during his first presidential campaign, and he always objected when other people offered it as a description of his convictions or ideals. He still routinely points out that the members of different racial populations tend in certain contexts to have different experiences, and that these differences are politically and ethically important. And he insists that this fact is compatible with the idea of a single American people, united by aspirations and ideals and history. So what does it mean that this man provided the occasion for a nation (and, in ways we'll come to in a later chapter, the world) to imagine the end of racial history? Where does he fit, if he fits, in the dynamically unfolding racial formation processes and contests of racial orders that frame the appeal to post-racialism?

As I've noted, Mr. Obama endorses neither the language of post-racialism nor the ideas that the language is often used to express. In his famous Philadelphia race speech, for example, he said the following:

> Contrary to the claims of some of my critics, black and white, I have never been so naïve as to believe that we can get beyond our racial divisions in a single election cycle, or with a single candidacy—particularly a candidacy as imperfect as my own.[27]

Explicit disavowals like this notwithstanding, Mr. Obama's public pronouncements and image management cut a distinctively post-racial figure. Put differently, in ways that are available to us in light of the discussion above: he explicitly refuses the simplest forms of post-racialism, but routinely speaks and acts in ways that align neatly with the imperatives of the colorblind racial project (for which, you'll recall, post-racialism provides the ideological content). This post-racial convergence is evident in at least three aspects of the president's public career.

First, Mr. Obama's deracializing electoral strategies were calculated to mesh with the colorblind ethos that has become our public political common sense. In speaking of deracialization, I have in mind Mr. Obama's mastery of the techniques that black candidates in majority-white settings have used in earnest since the

1990s, and that follow from a single, simple directive: "campaign in a . . . fashion that defuses the polarizing effects of race by avoiding explicit reference to race-specific issues."[28] This strategy makes non-white candidates more palatable to white voters, though not as much as one might think; and it has been wildly successful, if the careers of Deval Patrick and Cory Booker and Mia Love, and in a different way, of Nikky Haley, Bobby Jindal, and Mia Love, and in yet another way, of Condoleeza Rice, Clarence Thomas, and Colin Powell, are any indication.

The problem with deracialization is that it does its work by acceding to the imperatives of the colorblind racial project, rather than, as some of its advocates and its critics suggest, by "smuggling" secretly race-conscious candidates into office, where they will then suddenly speak to the racial issues that they had to table in order to get elected. You'll recall that racial projects are double-barreled affairs, with discursive and material dimensions. The discursive side of the post-racial project denies the validity of explicit appeals to race and enshrines abstract colorblindness as our ethico-political commonsense. At the same time, on the material side, the racially asymmetric distribution of social goods proceeds apace, shielded from scrutiny by the insistence on color-blindness. Deracialization satisfies the discursive requirements of colorblindness with its commitment to race-neutral rhetoric, and it aligns with the material contours of the project by excluding from policy debates the issues that disproportionately affect black voters.[29]

A second point at which Mr. Obama's public career converges with post-racial imperatives emerges from his orientation to recent racial history. You'll recall from the introduction that "post-" talk tends to be an exercise in space-clearing and in marking the end-points of an historical period. The idea tends to be that something, some temporal movement, has come to a close, and has in the process made room for something new, something that we do not yet have the words to describe. For this reason, understanding and evaluating posterizing claims requires getting clear on just what they mean to clear away, and what they mean to make room for. So what is it that post-racialism means to transcend?

The key to figuring out which world post-racialism counsels us to quit may lie in figuring out what sustains the optimism that the next world is already in the making. As we've noted, the post-racial idea caught on in earnest after Mr. Obama established himself as a viable candidate for the US presidency. During this heady time, the airwaves and newsstands and RSS feeds were swamped with sentiments like the one expressed in this fairly representative article from *New Leader* magazine: "In the postracial era personified by Obama, *civil rights veterans of the past century are consigned to history* and Americans start to make race-free judgments about who should lead them" (Schorr 2008, p. 4). If we credit this sort of journalistic testimony (which exists in considerable abundance), it appears that the "post" in "post-racialism" means to distance us from the specific regime of racial practices that we typically connect with the civil rights movement.

The thought that the civil rights enterprise has become obsolete, moribund, or otherwise irrelevant requires more careful consideration than I can give it here. But my aim right now is not to evaluate the probity of the thought, but to suggest that some version of it is at the core of the colorblind racial project, and very near the core of Mr. Obama's understanding of the political position he must carve out and occupy. One way to develop the thought is to say that the era of racial politics may have been necessary, but that its aims have been achieved. Let's say, in the truncated way of thinking that Americans usually bring to these things, that this era stretched from 1955 to 1972, from the Montgomery bus boycott to the National Black Political Convention in Gary, Indiana. It may have been a stage we had to work through in order to finish off the Strom Thurmonds and reform the George Wallaces of the world. But now, since whites no longer concentrate their votes and other resources to keep non-whites disempowered, exploited, and exploitable in the manner of *de jure* white supremacy, there is no need for non-whites to line up presumptively behind leaders of their own race. We now vote and organize on the basis of shared interests rather than on the basis of complexion. And we know, by and large, that to do otherwise is to violate the principle, articulated most ably by Dr. King, that has become central to our shared public philosophy:

that we should judge people on the content of their character rather than on the color of their skin.

We have already considered a fair bit of evidence that the case for this post-civil rights triumphalism is rather severely overstated. Against the idea that we now vote on the basis of shared interests, Tesler and Sears point out that "[b]ehind [Mr. Obama's] success in the primaries and general election . . . lay perhaps the most racialized presidential voting patterns in American history."[30] And against the idea that non-whites no longer have their life chances systematically diminished, Martin and others offer their evidence for the "changing same" view of recent racial history.

Interestingly, though, the empirical warrant for post-racialism's philosophy of history has little to do with its cultural currency, or, as a result, with its political utility. In a number of ways that we don't have space to explore here, it is important to many people, and to many US social interests, to believe that we have transcended race and racial politics, and, as a result, that people like Jesse Jackson are relics of a bygone era. For all of these same reasons and more besides, it is important for deracializing black politicians to signal that they fit into this new conception of our place in racial time. As a result, they fashion themselves into post-black politicians, "who have relatively few connections with organic black social and political formations and institutions, and consciously minimize their identity as 'minority' or 'black.'"[31] The journalistic evidence of Mr. Obama's commitment to this strategy is legion, so a few gestures should suffice to make the point. First there is Mr. Obama's arms-length relationship to established spaces for black public deliberation, like his at-the-time controversial decision to skip Tavis Smiley's State of the Black Union gathering in 2008.[32] Then there is his eagerness to adopt the "Sister Souljah" strategy,[33] publicly demonstrating his willingness to deliver "tough love" to black audiences in ways that seem calculated to win approval from non-black observers. Examples include Mr. Obama's peculiar culture of poverty addresses before *college graduates* at Morehouse in 2013, and, even more strangely, before the Congressional Black Caucus in 2011.[34] Finally, there is the way Mr. Obama positions himself relative to the civil rights enterprise, when he bothers to do so at all. He routinely describes himself and his listeners as members of "the Joshua generation," in a move that efficiently and effectively uses biblical references to locate his place in racial time—a place after the "Moses generation" of civil rights leaders like Jackson. Journalist David Remnick explains the move eloquently, pointing out that Obama's use of this trope in his first presidential campaign

> posed Obama himself as the break with history, the focal point of a new era, embracing America itself for all its tribes, for all its historical enmities and possibilities. In effect, it congratulated the country for getting behind him. Wright, Jackson—they were leaders of the old vanguard. Obama would lead the new vanguard, the Joshua generation.[35]

A final point of convergence between post-racial imperatives and Mr. Obama's public persona emerges from his embrace of the post-racial, post-civil rights philosophy of history. According to that philosophy, the civil rights movement, or our consolidation of the gains of that movement, breaks history into before and after. It creates an opening for new modes of political mobilization, social affiliation, cultural practice, and self-conception. On one way of extending that philosophy, we can't say what this new world looks like apart from specifying its point of departure because there is nothing else in the relevant register of discourse or domain of practice to do the work that we wanted the race concept to do. Civil rights-style identity politics was the last gasp of race-thinking and racial practice, and with the collapse of that political model we have reached the end of racial history. We are post-racial—inhabitants of a condition we can specify only by appeal to our point of departure—because we can now set off in different directions, unified only in our refusal to follow paths laid out by the shibboleths of race-thinking.

On this "end of history" version of the posterizing move, what comes next, after whatever it is we've transcended, is a kind of freedom. The enterprise that has reached the end of its history does not stop; it just continues without the burden of moving history forward, and without the constraints that limited it before. For Marx, the end of economic history does not mean the end of allocating resources and engaging in productive activity; it means freedom from the alienation of capitalism's specialized routines, freedom "to hunt in the morning, fish in the afternoon, rear cattle in the evening, criticise after dinner, just as I have a mind, without ever becoming hunter, fisherman, herdsman or critic."[36] For post-historical artists, on Charles Taylor's reading of Hegel, the end of the history of art doesn't mean the end of art-making; it means that artists can do their work unencumbered by external burdens like realistic representation, leaving them free to explore "the adventures of fantasy."[37]

By extension, for post-historical racial figures, the end of racial history doesn't mean that racial meanings cease to circulate in society. It just means that tasks like identity formation, culture making, and coalition building can be newly playful and open-ended, freed from the burdens of representing or uplifting the race, or authentically participating in its group life. This means that artists like Dave Chappelle can play with racial meanings in ways that would once have been taboo, and that politicians like Barack Obama can tailor their public performances to their audiences, lapsing into "the familiar cadences and syntax of the black church" in some settings,[38] while playing it straight in others. More than this, it means that Obama's handlers can adopt strategies that reporters can summarize with words like these: "If black voters want to claim him as the black candidate, fine. If voters wanted to see him as biracial or post-racial, that was fine, too."[39]

CONCLUSION

Barack Obama never claimed to be ushering in the post-racial utopia. He and his handlers were happy enough, for a time, to let people read him as the herald of racial history's demise, if anyone was so inclined. But neither the president nor his people ever explicitly endorsed post-racialism, or any of the sentiments entailed by the obvious casual understandings of the post-racial idea.

Mr. Obama readily concedes, even in the context of otherwise disappointing public statements (like his response to the grand jury decision in Ferguson, Missouri, to which we will return at the end of this book), many of the points that make post-racialism a non-starter for many people. Racism remains a problem, he'll say. The accumulated weight of racial injustice over time still bears down on us even in the absence of any conscious intent to discriminate or oppress, and despite the real progress we have made in creating a more just, more egalitarian society. And Americans of all colors still let race-based assumptions hem in their attitudes toward their fellow citizens, toward options for public policy and candidates for public office, and toward the prospects for a unified nation.

At the same time, though, the president and his people have always been, and still remain, careful to keep his public actions and statements aligned, by and large, with the recent turn from civil rights discourse to colorblindness. He relies heavily on the techniques of deracialization and of post-black politics, both of which undermine the ability of black counter-publics to influence policy debates or public opinion. He cautiously keeps the icons and institutions of traditional black politics at arm's length, and positions himself less as an heir of this politics than as its annulment. And he willingly teases out different strands of his own complicated racial identity in performances for different audiences, in the process affirming those who take the permeability and messiness of racial boundaries as reason to abandon racial discourse altogether—or to argue that nowadays, anyone can be anything they want.

To make this last point is to come very near to saying that race no longer matters. Mr. Obama has of course never said this, and has expressly denied it. But the public philosophy recommended by the colorblind racial project takes something like this as its central claim. Race matters only negatively from the perspective of the colorblind ethos, as a way of marking something that we are barred, always and everywhere, from taking seriously into account. We can take account of it playfully, as when we marvel at the boundary-crossing spectacle of a white Australian woman rapping in the Dirty South style, or of Japanese women winning Jamaican dancehall dance competitions—or of black people dancing to black music at presidential inaugural balls. But serious engagements with the lasting significance of race are out of bounds, and have been put there by the same double-dealing strategy—say race matters, but act in ways that render it inert—that so often seems to shape President Obama's public persona.

NOTES

1 Chideya, Farai, "The State of the Post-Racial Union," in Gregory Parks, and. Matthew Hughey, Eds., *The Obamas and a (Post) Racial America?* Series in Political Psychology. (New York: Oxford University Press, 2011), 243–244, 243.

2 David Remnick, "The Joshua Generation," *The New Yorker*, November 17, 2008, accessed August 13, 2012 at www.newyorker.com/reporting/2008/11/17/0811 17fa_fact_remnick

3 "How Barack Obama can become our first postracial President," by Michael Meyers, November 15, 2008, accessed June 8, 2012 at www.nydaily news.com/opinion/barack-obama-postracial-president-article-1.338003

4 Jann S. Wenner, "Ready for the Fight: Rolling Stone Interview with Barack Obama," *Rolling Stone* April 25, 2012, accessed September 4, 2012 at www.rollingstone.com/politics/news/ready-for-the-fight-rolling-stone-inter view-with-barack-obama-20120425#ixzz25YejoNfF

5 Bakari Kitwana, "Between Expediency and Conviction: What We Mean When We Say 'Post-Racial,'" in T. Denean Sharpley-Whiting, Ed., *The Speech: Race and Barack Obama's "A More Perfect Union,"* (New York: Bloomsbury, 2009), 85–101, 87.

6 Kitwana, 2009, pp. 87–88.

7 William Julius Wilson, *The Declining Significance of Race: Blacks and Changing American Institutions* (Chicago, IL: University of Chicago Press, 1980); for his repudiation of the political upshot of the declining significance argument, *see* William Julius Wilson, "Why Obama's Race Speech Is a Model for the Political Framing of Race and Poverty," in Sharpley-Whiting 2009, 132–141.

8 Michael Tesler and David O. Sears, *Obama's Race: The 2008 Election and the Dream of a Post-Racial America* (Chicago, IL: University of Chicago Press, 2010), Kindle edition, Kindle Locations 1964–1965.

9 Tesler and Sears, 2010, Kindle Locations 1968–1972.

10 Martin p. 71, citing Amiri Baraka, "The Changing Same (Rhythm and Blues and New Black Music)," in Addison Gayle, Ed., *The Black Aesthetic* (New York: Anchor Books, 1971), 112–125.

11 Martin, 71.

12 Michele Alexander, *The New Jim Crow* (pub info); see also Greg Thomas, [info].

13 Desmond King and Rogers Smith, "Racial Orders in American Political Development," in Joseph Lowndes, Julie Novkov, and Dorian T. Warren, Eds., *Race and American Political Development* (New York: Routledge, 2008), 80–105.

14 King and Smith, 81.

15 King and Smith, 81.

16 King and Smith, 93.

17 King and Smith, 85.

18 King and Smith, 92.

19 *See* Cheryl Harris, "Whiteness as Property," *Harvard Law Review* 106:8 (1993), 1707–1791.

20 Cornel West, "The Prophetic Tradition in Afro-America," *Prophetic Fragments* (Trenton, NJ: Africa World Press/Grand Rapids, MI: Wm. B. Eerdmans, 1988) 38–49, 38.

21 Shelby Steele, A Bound Man: Why We Are Excited About Obama and Why He Can't Win (New York: Free Press, 2008).

22 Bonilla-Silva (2006) developed this line of argument in relation to ideologies of colorblindness and conceptions of post-civil rights politics well before the language of post-racialism came into vogue.

23 Stephen Steinberg (1995). Steinberg borrows the term from Daniel Patrick Moynihan, who in some ways provided the blueprint for its application to US racial politics (though that wasn't what he was talking about when he coined the expression).

24 *Parents Involved in Community Schools v. Seattle School District, 551 U.S. 701* (2007), p. 748.

25 Parents Involved, p. 835. This language comes from Justice Stephen Breyer's dissent.

26 William James, The Will to Believe and Other Essays in Popular Philosophy (1897; New York: Dover, 1956).

27 Barack Obama, "A More Perfect Union," in T. Denean Sharpley-Whiting, Ed., *The Speech: Race and Barack Obama's "A More Perfect Union,"* (New York: Bloomsbury, 2009), 237–252, 246. *See also* his "word of caution" about "postracial politics" in *The Audacity of Hope* (New York: Crown, 2006), 232.

28 Frederick Harris, *The Price of the Ticket* (New York: Oxford University Press, 2012), 147; citing Joseph McCormick and Charles E. Jones, "Deracialization Revisited: Thinking Through a Dilemma," in Georgia A. Persons, Ed., *Dilemmas of Black Politics: Leadership, Strategy, and Issues* (New York: HarperCollins, 1993), 77.

29 *See* Harris 137–169.

30 Tesler and Sears, Kindle location 1971–1972.

31 Carly Fraser, "Race, Postblack Politics, and the Candidacy of Barack Obama," in Manning Marable and Kristen Clarke, Eds., *Barack Obama and African American Empowerment* (New York: Palgrave, 2009), 165.

32 Taylor Marsh, "Obama Ducks State of the Black Union," *Huffington Post*, posted May 25, 2011, accessed November 27, 2014 at www.huffingtonpost.com/taylor-marsh/obama-ducks-state-of-the-_b_88126.html

33 The strategy derives its name from Bill Clinton's famous harangue—delivered before Jesse Jackson's Rainbow Coalition—against rapper and writer Lisa "Sister Souljah" Williamson.

34 Richard Prince, "Obama, Blacks, and Personal Responsibility," *The Root*, posted May 22, 2013, accessed November 27, 2014 at www.theroot.com/blogs/journal isms/2013/05/obamas_2013_morehouse_speech_whats_his_personal_respons ibility_to_blacks.html; Nathan McCall, "At the Congressional Black Caucus, Obama's Sister Souljah Moment," *The Washington Post*, 30 September 2011, accessed November 27, 2014 at www.washingtonpost.com/opinions/at-the-con gressional-black-caucus-obamas-sister-souljah-moment/2011/09/30/gIQAKoE 9AL_story.html

35 David Remnick, "The Joshua Generation," *The New Yorker*, November 17, 2008, accessed August 13, 2012 at www.newyorker.com/reporting/2008/11/17/0811 17fa_fact_remnick, p. 5.

36 Karl Marx and Friedrich Engels, The German ideology: with selections from parts two and three, together with Marx's "Introduction to a critique of political economy" (1845; London: Lawrence and Wishart, 1970), 54.

37 Charles Taylor, *Hegel* (New York: Cambridge University Press, 1975), 478.

38 Remnick 4.

39 Tesler and Sears, Kindle locations 109–110, citing Evan Thomas, *A Long Time Coming: The Inspiring Combative 2008 Campaign and the Historic Election of Barack Obama* (New York: Public Affairs, 2009), 71.

Two

INTRODUCTION

While Barack Obama never explicitly claimed to be the harbinger of the post-racial era, he did routinely seize opportunities to present racial divisions as unfortunate but defeasible barriers to national unity. The rhetorical apex of the speech that first brought Mr. Obama to the attention of most people in the US, his keynote address to the 2004 Democratic national convention, eloquently sounded this theme in ways that he would echo many times in the years to come. "There's not a black America and white America and Latino America and Asian America," he said. "There's the United States of America."[1]

Values like unity, consensus, harmony, and reconciliation appear central to Mr. Obama's sense of his calling. Building consensus, healing wounds, closing divisions: all of these seem central both to his vision of himself as a public figure and to his diagnosis of what ails democracy in the US. We can see that this goes beyond race and ethnicity in the passages immediately surrounding the "black and white America" line.

> [A]longside our famous individualism, there's another ingredient in the American saga, a belief that we are all connected as one people. . . . [That belief] allows us to pursue our individual dreams, yet still come together as a single American family: "E pluribus unum," out of many, one. Now even as we speak, there are those who are preparing to divide us, the spin masters and negative ad peddlers who embrace the politics of anything goes. Well, I say to them

tonight, there's not a liberal America and a conservative America; there's the United States of America. . . . The pundits, the pundits like to slice and dice our country into red states and blue States: red states for Republicans, blue States for Democrats. But I've got news for them, too. We worship an awesome God in the blue states, and we don't like federal agents poking around our libraries in the red states.[2]

This commitment to political unity—to the pursuit of, as he put it in the line that became the title for his Philadelphia race speech, "a more perfect union"—informs Mr. Obama's famous insistence on compromise and centrism. When he took office, he genuinely seemed to think, to the dismay of more cynical observers of federal politics, that compromise was possible, and that overtures to his political opponents would build trust and promote reciprocity. Some of these cynical observers argued that the president's refusal to get tougher on his opponents was a reflection of some more worrisome reality. For some it reflected his deep aversion to conflict and his tendency to engage, as Gary Wills memorably put it, in "omnidirectional placation."[3] For others it was a function of simple incompetence or inexperience. For still others it had to do with the considerable common ground that Obama shared with the Republicans, on issues from health care reform (Obamacare began its life as Romneycare, though both major parties seemed to have agreed to ignore this fact) to the general advisability of market solutions to social problems.

These various diagnoses of Mr. Obama's fascination with compromise and unity are not mutually exclusive, but I don't propose to sort through them here. My aim is to consider some of the ways in which an expressly philosophical attempt at diagnosis plays out. Many people, including many who are not academic philosophers, decided that the way to explain Mr. Obama's emphasis on conciliation and unity was to read him as a philosophical pragmatist, in the mold of people like John Dewey and William James. Many fewer people, as far as I could tell, thought that this was an odd way to go. I am in the second group, for reasons that I'll use this chapter to explain.

The explanation will get fully underway after some preliminary exercises in stage setting. The first will offer some words on what pragmatism is supposed to mean in what follows. After a section rehearsing some arguments for the idea of Obama's pragmatism, another bit of stage setting will encroach a bit on my early promise to refrain from evaluating Obama administration policies, and from weighing Mr. Obama's assertions against the facts. This encroachment will turn out to be necessary because a recurring feature of the Obama-as-pragmatist line is the invocation of Deweyan conceptions of intelligence and inquiry. This move puts questions of truth, or better, of truth-*seeking*, on the table, and requires that we say something about Mr. Obama's manifest orientation to the work of social inquiry, as revealed in his public problem-solving activities. So it will be necessary to say something about what those activities look like.

With the preliminaries out of the way, the way will be clear to take up the main questions. What exactly does Mr. Obama's alleged pragmatism involve? Is it a useful way to understand either this president or his claims to post-partisanship? And what does this perhaps-pragmatic orientation to politics mean for democratic life?

WHAT PRAGMATISM MEANS HERE

There are, famously, many different ways to define pragmatism, and many versions to account for once the definition is in place. It is not crucial for present purposes that we sort through the various options with maximum care. It will be enough to get clear on the stakes of distinguishing philosophical pragmatism from its vernacular relatives, and on what the people who see Mr. Obama as a philosophical pragmatist think they are seeing.

The best way to start is to fix ideas around the main vernacular— which is to say, non-philosophical—versions of pragmatism. There is first of all the garden-variety sense of the term that we find in everyday, non-technical uses of the English language. In this sense, a pragmatist is just someone for whom abstract considerations of theory or principle are less important than the immediate pressures of getting things done. We see this conception at work in the way close aides describe Mr. Obama, as when Valerie Jarrett says, "I'm not sure people understand how pragmatic he is. He's a pragmatist. He really wants to get things done."[4]

A second, distinctly political sense of the term grows out of this first one. On this second usage, a pragmatist is someone who privileges compromise over conviction, who prefers political victories to principled losses. This is the sense in which *The Hill* reports that the common beltway perception of Rahm Emanuel, Mr. Obama's chief of staff at the time, was "as a political pragmatist, pushing Obama to accept realistic limitations . . . in order to secure smaller victories over abject failures."[5]

Chris Hayes, one of the most articulate spokespersons for the Obama-as-pragmatist line, explains the path from these vernacular conceptions of pragmatism to a more ambitious philosophical approach. On the D.C. beltway conception, he explains, "'pragmatic' is a kind of code word" for post-partisan and non-ideological.[6] But ideologies, properly understood, are inescapable. As no less an authority than Alan Greenspan points out, an ideology is just "a conceptual framework [that organizes] the way people deal with reality. Everyone has one. . . . The question is whether it is accurate or not."[7] The problem with vernacular pragmatism is that it either smuggles in its ideological commitments, or it eschews such commitments and leaves itself open to incoherence, gullibility, or passivity. At some point, decisionmakers have to make principled stands, even if they claim to be pragmatists. The key to this for Obama may involve embracing the expressly philosophical pragmatism that animates the career of his political hero, Abraham Lincoln.

> Pragmatism in common usage may mean simply a practical approach to problems and affairs. But it's also the name of the uniquely American school of philosophy whose doctrine is that truth is pre-eminently to be tested by the practical consequences of belief. What unites the two senses of the word is a shared skepticism toward certainties derived from abstractions—one that is welcome and bracing after eight years of a failed, faith-based presidency. Both senses

of the word . . . course through the life of Obama's hero, Abraham Lincoln.[8]

Philosophical pragmatism, then, has two main tenets, so far. Truth must somehow be related to practical consequences, and truth-seeking must embody a kind of "skepticism toward certainties derived from abstractions." Careless renderings of ideas like these have caused commentators no end of trouble, and launched some of them into utterly ludicrous readings of pragmatism's canonical figures. It will therefore pay us to take some care with this language, and to turn to some canonical figures in the pragmatist tradition for assistance.

To link truth to consequences just is to operationalize the skepticism about abstractions and certainty. Charles Sanders Peirce helpfully puts this in terms of the various methods of fixing belief and settling doubt. Sometimes we arrive at our beliefs by accepting what authorities tell us; sometimes by holding on to whatever we already happen to believe for all we're worth, and avoiding contact with countervailing arguments and evidence; and sometimes by rationally reflecting, in solitude or with others, on what seems most sensible to believe. But the method that has proven most fruitful in human history, and, not coincidentally, that is most likely to produce beliefs that actually track the way the world works, involves what we've come to think of as science: subjecting our beliefs to cross-examination in light of experience of the world outside our minds and our parlors, and accepting that this process may require adjusting our beliefs in light of the testimony of "rough facts."[9]

The relationship between truth and consequences is embodied, or epitomized, in the conclusions that scientists draw on the basis of their experiments. The conclusions are taken for truth, but provisionally. They count as truth, William James would later say, "in so far forth"—unless and until the results of later experiments force a reconsideration. The judgments that result from this process are provisional and fall short of the comforts of absolute certainty. But they can claim the status of truth more plausibly than the judgments that we generate by any of Peirce's other methods for fixing belief. And they are more likely to help us get around in a world of rough facts than the aspirant truths bequeathed to us by tradition, stubborn whim, or abstract reason.

On Hayes' account, borrowed on this point from Louis Menand, this experimentalist and fallibilist pragmatism recommended itself to the nineteenth-century classical pragmatists because it held out the promise of reconciliation.

> Having witnessed, and in some cases experienced firsthand, the horror of violence and irreconcilable ideological conflict during the Civil War, William James, Charles Peirce and Oliver Wendell Holmes were moved to reject the metaphysical certainty in eternal truths that had so motivated the abolitionists, emphasizing instead epistemic humility, contingency and the acquisition of knowledge through practice —trial and error.[10]

This refusal of certainty and embrace of contingency and experimentation has social and political implications. As contemporary political philosopher Robert Talisse puts it, to be a believer is to be committed to the requirements of proper inquiry, and "proper inquiry can be practiced only within a democratic political order."[11] Some years after Peirce and James, John Dewey developed a robust account of social life and education (and much else besides) based on these pragmatic principles, with the idea of democracy at its heart.

Another advocate for reading Mr. Obama as a pragmatist, Bart Schultz, usefully picks up the thread at this point and connects the dots from Lincoln through Dewey to Obama.

> What Obama has found in Lincoln just is what the pragmatists have always found in him, and this has been a type of pragmatism long associated with the University of Chicago. It is a vision of a democratic community as an educating community, as an experimental, open community of inquiry that through participation mobilizes our collective intelligence and problem-solving abilities.[12]

Pragmatic experimentalism, then, is not just a doctrine for scholars; it is a sensibility that informs the life of democratic communities. The commitment to democracy runs deep here, going beyond the formalities of voting and representation to embrace the faith that ordinary people can work together to grow, solve problems, and create the conditions for rewarding and mutually enriching experiences.

For current purposes, we'll have to set aside all of the technical disputes that philosophers might raise here. There are of course many different ways of reading key figures like Peirce and Dewey, and it is not obvious that reading all of these figures, and others, as pragmatists is more productive than misleading. In addition, there are of course questions about whether any of this is right, or makes sense, or tracks the way one ought to think about democracy, deliberation, inquiry, or truth. These are all interesting questions, more or less, but they are all beside the point right now.

The only issue under consideration here is whether President Obama can plausibly count as some variety of philosophical pragmatist. In order to evaluate that idea, we first have to understand it. And the simplest way to do that is to do what we've been doing: find the proponents of the view explaining what they mean, recruit some of their statements into a judicious summary, and expedite the work of summary where possible with language from canonical figures.

In light of the foregoing, we can say that pragmatists, in the sense of the term that seems to be in play for the Obama-as-pragmatist line, embrace four key convictions. First, the proper orientation to inquiry, including inquiry about social problems and policy, is a fallibilist experimentalism, rather than a dogmatic focus on a priori principles or eternal truths. Second, experimentalism is the appropriate posture in part because it improves the chances that our encounters with the world, our attempts to intervene in its operations to achieve our own ends, will be productive. Third, experimentalism is appropriate also because it minimizes the chances of conflict and disharmony, and creates space for conciliation and cooperation. And fourth, the commitment to experimentalism also requires a commitment to democracy, which is to say, to the cultivation of the spaces and capacities that allow open-ended inquiry to flourish among ordinary citizens. Call these "experimentalism," "voluntarism," "conciliation," and "thick democracy."

The clearest alternative to this pragmatic orientation to politics is the ideological, excessively principled approach that Hayes finds worrying contemporary denizens of Washington and that Menand finds worrying the classical pragmatists after the Civil War. But it is important to draw another contrast, one that is equally dangerous from this perspective. Schultz describes it in a discussion of the discursive conditions that obtained when the Deweyan account of democracy might have taken root at the University of Chicago.

> The University, like the country as a whole, was structured more in accordance with something like Walter Lippmann's elitist, managerial conception of limited democracy. Lippmann, who started out as a socialist, steadily moved to a more hierarchical conception of democracy, emphasizing how limited and gullible public opinion needed to be guided and constrained by various forms of elite expertise. He would play the top-down thinly democratic liberal to Dewey's bottom-up thickly democratic liberal, in a crucial philosophical duel that defined the options for American politics in the early twentieth century.[13]

This passage from Schultz makes clear that the pragmatism he champions, and that he finds Obama championing, means to ward off two threats. On one side are the ideologues, with their unearned and disempowering certainties, and their preference for abstract reason or unyielding faith over hard-won intelligence. But on the other side are the technocrats, with their elitist and unprincipled mistrust of the demos. As is often the case with pragmatists, Mr. Obama will have to chart a middle way through these extremes.

THE PRESIDENT AS PRAGMATIST

Given the picture of philosophical pragmatism assembled so far, does the president fit the bill? There are, to be sure, quite good reasons to link Mr. Obama to the pragmatist tradition, reasons that Schultz, Hayes, and others like Mitchell Aboulafia have made clear. For one thing, Mr. Obama makes the noises one expects a pragmatist to make. For another, he was raised, intellectually and politically, by people and in places that have been steeped in the ideas of Dewey and others. And finally, reading him as a pragmatist might make better sense of him than declining to do so.

One needn't dig deeply into Mr. Obama's writings and speeches to find him sounding like a pragmatist. Sometimes he embraces the label outright, as when he describes "his national security team as 'shar[ing] my pragmatism about the use of power.'"[14] Most of the time, though, the resonances are less direct, functioning more like echoes or evocations of classical pragmatist themes and rhetoric. For example, Mr. Obama could be channeling William James as he explains that reflecting on the fervent absolutisms of Garrison and Tubman left him "robbed of the certainty of uncertainty—for sometimes absolute truths may well be absolute."[15] In other places he sounds more like Dewey, according to Schultz, in his recurring emphasis on "democratic, progressive education . . . on bottom-up politics and community service, on democracy as a way of life or culture of deliberation and participation . . . [and] on experimentalism and fallibilism."[16] In still other places he goes beyond Dewey, or beyond the way Dewey is usually read, to incorporate more of the "cosmic sadness" that we find in Lincoln and in the broader Chicago pragmatist tradition.[17] But in all of these places he invokes recognizably pragmatist themes, and does so unambiguously.

In a similar spirit, Aboulafia points us to Obama's discussion of Sonia Sotomayor's nomination to the Supreme Court, in which the president uses Oliver Wendell Holmes to sound the themes of radical empiricism and faith in the demos that animate so much of the pragmatist tradition:

> [T]wo qualities [intellect and a sense of the judiciary's limits] are essential, I believe, for anyone who would sit on our nation's highest court. And yet, these qualities alone are insufficient. We need something more. For as Supreme Court Justice Oliver Wendell Holmes once said, "The life of the law

has not been logic; it has been experience." Experience being tested by obstacles and barriers, by hardship and misfortune; experience insisting, persisting, and ultimately overcoming those barriers. It is experience that can give a person a common touch and a sense of compassion; an understanding of how the world works and how ordinary people live. And that is why it is a necessary ingredient in the kind of justice we need on the Supreme Court.

(Aboulafia 2009, par. 6)

In light of this sort of documentary evidence, and in keeping with the principle of interpretive charity that enjoins us to assume, other things being equal, that people mean what they say, we should accept that Mr. Obama has with these statements committed himself to something at least in the vicinity of philosophical pragmatism.

We might be encouraged in reading Mr. Obama as a pragmatist, and in taking his Jamesian and Deweyan utterances at face value, that he was reared, intellectually, around and by pragmatists. Schultz makes this point quite forcefully in his detailed discussion of Mr. Obama's Chicago roots. The future president learned community organizing in the Alinsky school, which is explicitly Deweyan in its aims.[18] And he spent his politically formative years in and around the University of Chicago, which preserved and transformed the pragmatism of Dewey and Addams, and passed it on to Mr. Obama and others (including Obama's political advisor, David Axelrod), by way of figures like neglected political scientist David Greenstone and legal scholar Cass Sunstein. Here is Schultz's helpful summary of this argument:

Has Obama actually read Greenstone? Allen? Rorty? At one level, it scarcely matters. Just as his daughters, as students at the Lab Schools, absorb Deweyanism as a matter of course, the intellectual air he breathed both as an organizer and at the University was simply filled with these ideas—ideas that one of his leading advisors, Cass Sunstein, was directly involved in developing.

(Schultz 2009, 170)

Finally, we might credit Mr. Obama's rearing in a pragmatist environment as formative because doing so gives us an interpretive frame that makes more sense of him than some obvious alternatives do. I think here of the arguments that Aboulafia and Hayes have offered against the claim that Obama is a vulgar pragmatist, valuing expediency over principle, concrete solutions over abstract ideology. Aboulafia makes the point quite clearly:

> Failure to understand that Obama is a philosophical prag-matist, as opposed to simply a political one, explains much of the confusion about his approach to selecting nominees and advisers. When Obama talks about the importance of experience, when he talks about consequences (as opposed to abstract principles), when he talks about fallibilism, when he talks about consultation and cooperation, and when he talks about what works, he is using well known catch phrases of this tradition. And he knows it. Unfortunately, political commentators, left, right and center, don't.
>
> (Aboulafia 2009, par. 2)

I'm not entirely sold on these arguments, in part for reasons I'll soon come to, and in part because, as the late Mike Eldridge put it on the web page that helpfully anchored much of the early discussion of this issue among philosophers, "I don't know what Obama knows."[19] But they are worth a conversation, and certainly worth the time and effort their authors have put into them. We might quibble over just how to read Obama's words, and over the degree to which pragmatist commitments saturated the environment in which the future president found his intellectual bearings. We might quibble further by saying that the label is easy, that there are many different kinds of pragmatism, and that the devil is in the details that distinguish one kind from another. But I'll leave that work to someone else—or most of it, at any rate. I want to consider instead what becomes of the claim that Obama is a pragmatist even if we accept these arguments. These are, as I've said, reasons for linking him to the tradition; but it isn't obvious that recogniz-ing these links means assenting to assertions like "Obama is a pragmatist." Nor is it obvious that these assertions are the best way of crediting the links, or that extending this credit is their only or even their primary function.

SUSPECTING THE QUESTION

If the only options are to assent to or dissent from the Obama-as-pragmatist thesis, I choose dissent. There may be bad reasons for this—call these, generously, grounds for being suspicious of the question—and it is important to make these clear at the outset, in the interest of full disclosure. Then we can turn in more promising directions.

I do most of my work in the fields of Africana philosophy and race theory, and people there have for some reason grown fond of invoking something that they call "pragmatism" without much regard for the specifically philosophical resonances of the idea. For example: Tommie Shelby and Anna Stubblefield both argue for views (on nationalism and racialism, respectively) that they call pragmatic while explicitly distancing themselves from the prag-matist tradition. And they do this despite the fairly clear relevance of pragmatist philosophy to their interests in social theory and ethics. A little less distressingly, Bill Lawson ingeniously argues that Booker T. Washington is "the embodiment of the pragmatist tradi-tion," and worries that Cornel West included Du Bois in *American Evasion* without even mentioning the Wizard of Tuskegee.[20]

I admire this work, and I admire and like the people who do it. But it puts me in mind of Peirce's desire to invent a new name that's too ugly for kidnappers. And this is the source of one bad reason for resisting the idea of Obama's pragmatism: My encounter with counterfeit pragmatism in these other contexts has made me oversensitive to the possibility of devaluing the currency, of pretending that superficial invocations of the idea can do the same work as more robustly philosophical uses of it. I confess to taking umbrage at this devaluation, whether it derives from the vague sense that pragmatism resembles something we like (Washington's practical bent, among other things, though I confess to having come around to some of what Lawson is after lately), or whether it derives from an intramural parochialism that blinds us to viable philosophic resources (in Alain Locke, or in Royce) for advancing an ongoing inquiry. And I confess to bristling, perhaps preemptively, perhaps prematurely, at the sense that some version of this devaluation is in the offing with claims about Mr. Obama.

Of course, you now see why I describe this as a bad reason to worry about the Schultz–Aboulafia reading of the president. Their point is precisely that Obama's speeches and writings announce his immersion, his self-conscious immersion, accomplished over many years of his life, in the pragmatist tradition, and that his orientation to political work and to the burdens of governance are best understood in light of this tradition. So it is not inconsequential that he constantly invokes Lincoln, or that he occasionally evokes Dewey or Holmes, or that he seems to have passed through Dewey as surely and as momentously as Dewey says he passed through Hegel. It is not inconsequential that Obama puts before us the burdens of prospectively forging a shared political identity without recourse to primordial or transhistorical essences, and that he does this while insisting on the burdens of finding our normative bearings in a world with living histories instead of transcendent guarantees. These are pragmatist moves, and Obama clearly and eloquently makes them.

I begin with this bad reason for dissent not just in the interest of full disclosure, as I mentioned, but also because it begins to point us to the register of analysis that opens once we refuse the binary "is he or isn't he?" terms of debate. My bad reason for dissent requires diagnosis; it makes clear that my orientation to Mr. Obama, my inclination to answer the question of his pragmatism negatively, says at least as much about me, and my concerns, and the conditions of my inquiry, as it does about him. I will suggest near the end of this discussion that something like this is also true of the affirmative answer.

PRAGMATISM IN ACTION? SNAPSHOTS
OF POLICY AND POLITICS

Before we shift into a diagnostic, question-questioning mode, though, it is important to consider a second, better reason to respond negatively to the question of the president's pragmatism as it stands. The affirmative answer that we find in the Schultz–Aboulafia reading depends rather heavily on Mr. Obama's writings and speeches. This reading is also supposed to provide us with a key for understanding Mr. Obama's approach to governance—e.g., his willingness to experiment (like Lincoln), and his insistence on the importance of experience (traced to Holmes, worthy of Dewey) in, say, making nominations to the Supreme Court. But the key to the reading lies primarily in what this president has written and said, and in how we're given to understand those things in light of his immersion in spaces saturated by Deweyan ideas.

This is all very persuasive, to a point. But we may have moved beyond that point in January 2009, at which point the subject matter of our inquiry may have changed, or, as some would have it, begun to fully reveal itself. That is: as a writer, a law professor, and a more or less local public servant, Mr. Obama absolutely made the kinds of noises and inhabited the kinds of spaces that the Schultz–Aboulafia reading requires. (He did other things too, and made other noises. And the Obama-as-pragmatist line must obscure these. But so be it.) All this notwithstanding, the Barack Obama who serves as our 44th president, and who inhabits the Beltway after Clinton and Rove rather than Chicago after Dewey, seems a rather different animal, much less likely to make these noises, and much more likely to act in ways that pull against the import of making them.

Think for a moment about the issue of Lincolnian experi-mentation. It's one thing to be a fallibilist, to eschew foolish consistency and break rules, revise plans that have grown too narrow for the actual case. But the Deweyan manner of doing this, at least, has requirements, as we've seen. For one thing, it requires that one choose the course of action at the heart of the experiment *intelligently*, which is to say on the basis of the best information we have, gathered using the best methods we have. For another, it requires that we make these choices in the context of a political apparatus that credits and cultivates the capacities of ordinary people to deliberate responsibly and together about their shared problems and about the prospects for finding shared solutions. It is not in the least bit clear that this sort of democratic intelligence animates the Obama administration's policy experiments concerning Afghanistan, DADT (the "Don't Ask, Don't Tell" approach to the sexual orientation of US soldiers), the financial crisis, health care, and, among other things, global trade. The administration is stacked with intelligent people, but their collective efforts typically seem guided by considerations other than social intelligence in the sense that Dewey tirelessly called for. Lincoln cast about for leaders and strategies because he was looking for something that worked; Mr. Obama seems, on at least some occasions, to cast about for strategies without regard for what is likely to work—unless "work" means something other than "solving society's problems," as, in our current policymaking context, it almost surely does.

The point I'm on the verge of making here will be contentious, and its plausibility will depend on one's estimate of Obama's performance. This will in turn depend at least in part on one's sense of the universe of plausible policy options in particular domains, and on one's ideas about just how much we might ever expect public policy to achieve the condition of Deweyan intelligence. These issues are no less contentious and complex than the philosophical infighting that we sidestepped on the way to a working definition of "pragmatism." Still, the issues can't entirely be avoided if we're to deal seriously with the question in play here.

The question at issue is whether Mr. Obama's actions as president are consistent with reading him as a pragmatist. His words, written and spoken, are one thing; but presidents—pragmatic presidents, one assumes, more than most—are people of action, and their actions are at least as vital for understanding what really matters to them, what they really are, as are their words. For this reason, we will have to consider these actions somehow, despite the limitations of space that bar us from considering questions of detail in detail, and from accounting carefully for differences in basic ethical and social-theoretic commitment and perspective.

In order to accommodate these difficulties, I propose to offer four short sketches of policy interventions and political maneuvers in the Obama administration. Each description should be sufficiently gestural to pass muster with commentators of varying ideological backgrounds, which is to say that each should be compatible with a commentator drawing out the facts and developing a critique, or defense, in any of a variety of directions. I will try to remain agnostic between different conceptions of the politically possible and desirable, deviating from this rule only to do the work that calls forth these sketches: to compare the move in question with the pragmatist commitments enumerated above. The intervention or maneuver might be good politics, or the best choice from a set of bad options, or evidence that pragmatist commitments are incompatible with the burdens of statecraft. I will, for now, take no position on any of these questions (the third will reclaim our attention somewhat later). The only question at issue right now is whether the intervention or maneuver is the sort of thing we might expect from someone who is sincerely committed to philosophical pragmatism; or, in the alternative, whether a president who leads an administration that does these things can plausibly bear interpretation as a pragmatist.

To be clear: what follows should not just be an expression of my political disagreements with Mr. Obama. The claim is neither that pragmatist commitments make people virtuous nor that they are compatible with good politics (whatever that comes to). This is not the claim in no small part because pragmatist commitments are compatible with a variety of political postures and states of character. The claim that in fact animates what follows is conditional. If Mr. Obama is a pragmatist in the sense described above, then we should be able to expect or rule out certain courses of action from him, irrespective of whether any of these actions would be politically advisable, or whether they would align with my own, or anyone else's, preferred policy solutions. It will turn out that the president's actions are hard to reconcile with the picture we get from people like Schultz.

As it happens, I do think that a firmer commitment to certain pragmatic principles would make for better governance. But I will try to keep this thought in the background. I will do this in part by borrowing the language for my sketches from sources across the ideological spectrum. The burden in what follows will be to weigh the evidence provided in the four short cases against the four pragmatic commitments set out in the definition of pragmatism offered above: experimentalism, voluntarism, conciliation, and thick democracy.

Snapshot #1: At a 2009 town hall on health insurance reform, a member of the audience asked President Obama whether he still supported a plan for universal coverage, and whether this was consistent with private companies still having a role in the system. After distinguishing universal coverage from single-payer plans, Mr. Obama said the following: "I have not said that I was a single-payer supporter because, frankly, we historically have had an employer-based system in this country with private insurers, and for us to transition to a system like that . . . would be too disruptive. So what would end up happening would be, a lot of people who currently have employer-based health care . . . would suddenly find themselves dropped. . . . I would be concerned about the potential destructiveness of that kind of transition."[21]

Response #1: This is surely an example of conciliation, but at what cost? Chief of Staff Rahm Emanuel was in the Clinton White House when an earlier attempt at reform got scuttled by an unhappy health industry, and vowed not to let that happen again. So here we have vernacular pragmatism in play, finding a way to win, principle be damned. At our most generous we might think of this conciliation as a matter of principled compromise, rather than, say, as a matter of a party bureaucracy protecting its revenue stream. But it is very difficult to see it as consistent with an experimentalist sensibility. Employer-based insurance may be our tradition, but tradition is a repository of experiments, and there are plenty of reasons to think —to at least consider the possibility, and submit it to the deliberative settings that our democracy affords us—that our health care experiments have failed badly enough to recommend another course of action. Especially, it must be said, when the precluded course of action, a single-payer health system of the sort that other countries have tried with considerable (though not unalloyed) success, has been the subject of other policy experiments that we can study and learn from.

Worse, to read tradition only as a fetter and not as a store of experiences that might sometimes recommend a change of course is to embrace a crude, uninteresting, watered-down form of conservatism rather than a philosophical pragmatism. To say, as Mr. Obama and his team did, that alternatives to our tradition can't be put on the table—not that they can't be enacted, but that they can't even be considered for the purposes of negotiation—because to do so would disrupt the status quo is to refuse the tingling challenge of risk that comes with social experimentation. (It is also, more simply, to undermine one's negotiating position rather severely, which, once again, goes to the question of how much social intelligence is in play here.) If this preemptive bracketing of questions about how to proceed in light of decades of evidence is pragmatism, it's mid-career Rorty at his most breezily and blandly solidaristic. It is what Dewey called accommodation, rather than conciliation or experimental adaptation.

Snapshot #2: After Mr. Obama chose Emanuel as his chief of staff, tensions arose between the White House and the support base that had been assembled during the campaign. The friction was laid bare in August [of 2009] when Mr. Emanuel showed up at a weekly strategy session featuring liberal groups and White House aides. Some attendees said they were planning to air ads attacking conservative Democrats who were balking at Mr. Obama's health-care overhaul. "F—ing retarded," Mr. Emanuel scolded the group, according to several participants. He warned them not to alienate lawmakers whose votes would be needed on health care and other top legislative items. . . . The weekly strategy sessions where he made the remark, called the Common Purpose Project, are by invitation only, and participants are sworn to secrecy. Activists say it's a one-way conversation, with the White House presenting its views and asking liberals to refrain from public criticism. Ms. Hamsher, publisher of the *Fire Dog Lake* blog, calls the gatherings the "veal pen."[22]

> [I]t turns out that [former Obama campaign manager David] Plouffe was a chief advocate for bringing in . . . Emanuel. . . . He writes, using a baseball analogy: "Rahm was a five-tool political player: a strategist with deep policy expertise, considerable experience in both the legislative and executive branches, and a demeanor best described as relentless." Note

that nowhere in that vital skill-set is any sense of how to work with the largest volunteer base any presidential campaign has developed in history. Rahm Emanuel came up in politics the old-fashioned way; organizing and empowering ordinary people are the least of his skills.[23]

Response #2: The tensions between Emanuel and the increasingly alienated Obama base were mirrored by the tensions between, on the one hand, Mr. Obama's genuflections to the idea of deliberation and citizen empowerment and, on the other, his political machine's determination to control its supporters. The base was apparently meant to be a resource, available for calls to action at the appropriate moments but otherwise meant to keep quiet and do as instructed. This does not sound like thick democracy, or like cultivating and employing the citizenry's capacity for intelligent problem-solving.

Snapshot #3: After a leaked document revealed that the Obama administration signed a special pact to keep all documents relating to Trans-Pacific Free Trade Agreement (FTA) negotiations secret, a broad array of US groups . . . joined their global counterparts . . . in demanding an end to the secrecy surrounding the controversial negotiations. Twenty-two US labor, consumer, faith, environmental and human rights organizations—including the AFL-CIO, Sierra Club, Presbyterian Church (USA) and Public Citizen—sent a letter to US Trade Representative Ron Kirk calling on the US government to implement the administration's transparency pledges. . . . "The fact that negotiators have gone out of their way to execute a special secrecy agreement has made a lot of people wonder just what exactly they are so afraid the press, the public and Congress would see if there was openness," said Lori Wallach, director of Public Citizen's Global Trade Watch. "While executives from hundreds of corporations have been named 'official trade advisors' by the Obama administration and given access to the texts, the people whose lives would be most affected may never get to see what our negotiators are bargaining for—and bargaining away—until it's all over." . . . [N]one of the draft texts has been released despite President Barack Obama's promises that the Trans-Pacific FTA will usher in a new era of transparency in trade agreement negotiations. . . .[24]

Response #3: More clearly than in the other cases, there is real controversy about the advisability of the course of action that pragmatist commitments recommend here. Veterans of this sort of negotiation suggest, plausibly, that negotiating in public is virtually impossible, which makes secrecy of some kind essential. With that said, there is something peculiar, and unpragmatic, in the way some stakeholders—business executives—get privileged access to the documents while other stakeholders do not—such as representatives from labor, if no one else, and the overmatched lawmakers who may receive the documents but are barred from sharing them with experts who might help them make sense of what they're reading. Once again, we seem to be working at cross-purposes to the idea of democratic, collaborative inquiry, and flouting the voluntarist injunction to promote the capacity of the demos to solve its own problems. Worse, we seem, as in the case of health insurance reform, to be drawing perilously close to Lippman's conception of elite technocratic rule, and leaving behind the thick democracy that Mr. Obama was supposed to have internalized during his time in Chicago.

Snapshot #4: An independent investigative journalist wrote the following in a January 2014 report on US policy concerning unmanned drone strikes:

> Since Obama's inauguration in 2009, the CIA has launched 330 strikes on Pakistan—his predecessor, President George Bush, conducted 51 strikes in four years. . . . The escalation in the drone war has happened with almost no official transparency from the White House. It took Obama three years to publicly mention his use of drones. In January 2012 he said "actually drones have not caused a huge number of civilian casualties." He added: "For the most part they have been very precise, precision strikes against al Qaeda and affiliates." In this period Bureau records show drones reportedly killed at least 236 civilians—including 61 children. And according to a leaked CIA record of drone strikes, seen by the McClatchy news agency, the US often did not know who it was killing.[25]

At a congressional hearing shortly after the release of the report,

> Rep. Adam B. Schiff (D-Calif.) urged intelligence officials
> . . . to release aggregate data each year on how many people
> the United States had killed in counterterrorism operations
> and how many might be civilians. Officials showed scant
> enthusiasm for the proposal. CIA Director John Brennan said
> it was a "worthwhile recommendation" that the administration
> could consider, but he declined to comment on it further.[26]

Response #4: It nearly goes without saying that conducting military operations without public comment for years is in tension with the idea of cultivating space for open-ended democratic inquiry—inquiry into the actions that the state ostensibly takes in the name of its people. It surely goes without saying that killing people without knowing whom one is killing—that doing anything without bothering to track an important consequence of the action— is in tension with the commitment to intelligent action.

I'll say once more, for the sake of clarity, that the point of these snapshots is not to catch Mr. Obama in violation of campaign promises, though there is some of that; nor is it to complain that he is governing badly, though I would say there's some of that too. Modern politics may just be the kind of affair that requires lying to voters, or, more generously, changing one's tune once one gets into office and discovers how things really work. In the same spirit, each of the courses of action canvassed above might be an instance of good policy and astute politics. I make no claims about any of those considerations. The point here is just that the actions noted above seem clearly to be in tension with the pragmatic commitments that people were once keen to project onto Mr. Obama. He may have made the right noises in his writings and speeches. But as the chief executive and commander in chief, his actions have drowned out his words.

Interestingly, the one pragmatic commitment that runs the gauntlet of the cases above and gets through unscathed is the conciliation imperative. The Obama administration routinely works to find common ground, avoid conflict, and promote harmony—but only with

Lippman's technocrats and elites, not with the demos. And it privileges this partial, hierarchical conception of harmony over rigorous experimentation or intelligent problem-solving.

What we see in these cases is not conciliation worthy of Lincoln, but compromise turned into a fetish, and a willingness to subordinate the (apparent) results and sites of small-d-democratic mobilization to the rituals and requirements of the beltway. If this is right, then one of the motivations for identifying Mr. Obama as a pragmatist loses some of its force. Part of the aim of moving from vernacular pragmatism to the philosophical variety was to reframe accusations of rudderlessness, of a preference for expediency over principle, as expressions of *philosophical* principle and fallibilist experimentation. But at some point what looks like expediency might just be expediency.

OBJECTIONS AND REPLIES

An obvious response to the worries raised above is that *Mr. Obama is the president*, for goodness' sake, which means that he has to deal with the real sources of political power, and that this severely curtails the space for noble or otherwise virtuous action. The financial services industry and the health insurance industry and so on are (among) the sources of power, and a president can't deal responsibly with them while pretending that they are no more powerful or influential than, say, the prostrate forces of labor and the unformed might of ordinary citizens.

This response presupposes that Mr. Obama has been prevented from doing things he wanted to do, which is not at all clear just in light of his openly avowed centrist sensibilities. But assuming this is right, the response also ignores the possibility that one of the president's jobs, as the beloved Lincoln knew, was to help set the national agenda, to use the power of the office—an expressive power that has grown exponentially since Lincoln's day—to reframe issues and help us—the demos—reorganize our sense of the possibility space, and invade that space productively. But if we set that aside too, there is still this to say: *Perhaps it's impossible to be both a philosophical pragmatist and a US president (after, say, Eisenhower, in any case)*. This objection essentially rehearses the Schumpeterian conception of democracy, which is precisely at odds with the Deweyan conception that was being claimed for Mr. Obama. If the defense of Obama's pragmatism is that democracy just is the name we give to the process whereby we occasionally subject elite rule to a kind of plebiscite, after which this rule goes its own way until the people have their next opportunity to register or withhold their approval, then Dewey and Chicago are well lost and the Obama-as-pragmatist game is up.

A slightly less obvious response, and one that started to peek through the first rejoinder, is that the president's pragmatic orientation is at work on a very deep level, which of course escapes the ability of ordinary folks like us to discern or understand. This means that policies that seem poorly tailored to their objectives actually have *hidden* objectives that only the ruler can properly see and evaluate. And the obvious counter to this is that *when we started Obama was a pragmatist, and now he's a caricature of Leo Strauss. Surely something has gone amiss.*[27]

The invocation of Strauss may seem too dramatic, since of course the president, being the president, has to accommodate himself to political realities that people on the outside just can't see. But it is not clear how much this difference—between a faux-Straussian exoteric writer and whatever Mr. Obama is supposed to be now—really makes a difference. The cost of holding on to the thought that the president really is or believes something that he is prevented from being or acting on just is the insistence on a peculiar form of opacity that insulates the chief executive from normal mechanisms of evaluation and democratic accountability. For these and other reasons, political commentators have been increasingly warming to the thought for which Adolph Reed and a few others laid the groundwork before the 2008 elections: that Mr. Obama hasn't been prevented from doing much of anything, that he has in fact done exactly what he wanted to do, pursuant to a politics that has more to do with protecting certain structures and interests as they stand than with intelligently solving social problems. This strikes me as much more likely than that his Deweyan tendencies have just gone into hiding.

From here a couple of related lines of argument become visible, related less to the issue of intelligence in social policy than to the burdens of democratic life. The Schultz–Aboulafia reading tells us that Obama's Lincolnian pragmatism, nurtured during his time in Dewey's old haunts, leads him to treat social life as a matter of forging identities rather than of piously reflecting antecedent truths. We forge these identities through civic education and manage their conflicts through conjoint deliberation, relying on hard-won common understandings rather than relying on such things as shared descent or biology as the basis for social cohesion.

But the White House has overseen precious little identity-forging and civic education since 2009. Teachable moments—on DADT (the "Don't Ask, Don't Tell" approach to the sexual orientation of US soldiers), on building labor protections into trade agreements, on the moral dimensions of financial markets, and much more—keep going by the wayside, as conventional beltway wisdom keeps animating the policy and politics. The mobilized democratic publics that helped win the election (if one buys that story; not everyone does) have been relegated to the sidelines. And the search for common ground has given way to poorly negotiated compromises (if they are that) with opponents who actively deny the value and refuse the possibility of shared understanding. If this is pragmatism, it abandons the fighting creed that Dewey and James called for and instead embodies some of the worst anti-pragmatic stereotypes— of Dewey's heirs as capitalist dupes, bereft of ethical convictions, building a politics of accommodation atop a philosophical psychology of piecemeal and passive adjustment.[28]

The standard evidence for this appeal to the forging of civic identities is Mr. Obama's deft handling of racial controversies. The "More Perfect Union" speech, for example, is widely regarded as a remarkable rhetorical achievement, and as a condensed version of the racial reconciliation that the Obama campaign, and the Obama cultural phenomenon, promised and to some degree achieved in a nation of deep-seated racial antipathies. But we saw in Chapter 1 that Mr. Obama's post-racial appeals dovetail neatly with a colorblind racial project, with unfortunate implications for democratic life that we can now make explicit.

The post-racial sleight of hand consists substantially in removing social problems from the domain of democratic deliberation and experimental problem solving. Instead of dealing with, say, the legacies of centuries of racially circumscribed mechanisms for wealth accumulation, we retreat to abstract principles—property rights, personal responsibility, or in the limit case, state's rights—and treat racially asymmetric stores of social, material, and cultural capital as natural phenomena. Similarly: instead of thinking in a fallibilist and experimental spirit about what a robust anti-racism would require, we turn Martin King into a caricature and turn one line from one speech—the "content of their character" line—into a self-executing, context-independent moral principle.

Perhaps worst of all: in its determination to assign the civil rights movement to the benighted time before our own, the post-racial sensibility requires and reinforces a narrow, highly tendentious picture of twentieth-century anti-racist struggle. To break US racial and anti-racist history into before and after Obama, to read the present as the culmination, completion, and transcendence of the civil rights movement, as the colorblind project typically does and as the machinery that generates Mr. Obama's public persona usually declines to contest, is precisely to miss an opportunity for the forging of new civic identities in a properly post-racial spirit.

The missed opportunity that I have in mind will become clearer once we fix ideas around the picture of the US anti-racist history I have in mind. Civil rights historians have in recent years developed a variety of powerful criticisms of the way the mid-century US racial justice struggles register in popular consciousness and public discourse. These popular narratives and images recommend to us the following erroneous ideas about "The Movement."

- Martin King was the preeminent and unquestioned leader (actually, he was in important ways led by it as often as he led it).
- There was a single movement to lead (actually, ideological and place-based variations in movement aims and strategies had a

great deal to do with King's inability to get out in front of, or even work productively with, every group or campaign).

- It was principally a protest movement (instead of, as activists often explicitly said, a movement aimed at securing human rights, or cultivating the capacity and creating the space for self-determination, or to demand the provision of basic services, and so on).
- The federal government was generally sympathetic (instead of sometimes working actively with racist reactionaries, sometimes with lethal effect, and in any case having to be prodded into action by activist campaigns that strategically put more valuable White lives—those of brave and sympathetic student volunteers—in the path of violence with their black colleagues).
- The movement ended when blacks turned from non-violent protest to rage-filled separatism and gave up on America (instead of this: contributors to the movement adapted in different ways to changing conditions, or to the nation's persistent refusal of their vision for change, or to the persistence and transformations of White supremacy, or to the demands of the diverse, multigenerational liberation movement that began well before the familiar starting point in 1955).

Why does this highly tendentious and misleading picture of US anti-racist struggle matter? Why, in particular, does it matter for Mr. Obama's alleged pragmatist and post-partisan aspirations? It matters first of all because the picture conveys a severely truncated sense of democratic agency, a sense that is rather profoundly at odds with the pragmatic commitments that Barack Obama the writer endorses. On this picture, one man hauls a nation out of moral backwardness while in the grip of a single, universally shared moral vision. Everyone falls into line behind him, until together— that is, with the followers following orders—they reveal to the nation the error of its ways and things change. And the people who refuse to sign off on the resulting new dispensation can be written off, or have written themselves off, as cranks and hence play no role in the ongoing democratic conversation.

The real picture, the picture that more faithfully reflects the dynamics of anti-racist struggle and of politics under the first black president, is more complicated. There are many leaders, and they contend with each other and with their followers to find the path forward. This contention can be made productive if leadership is widely distributed, and its capacities widely cultivated, among the first picture's mass of followers—as SNCC, in its best moments, saw during its local southern campaigns. Even success will be messy, and it will probably not involve univocal agreement about means or ends. Nor will it involve the state or, as we said in the previous chapter, the participants in the dominant racial order, simply accepting that they have been wrong. There will be violence and strife. And there will still, at the end, be people who do not recognize the success as a success.

The persistence of disagreement, even after the achievement of what appears to be ethical progress, points to the second reason our civil rights mythology matters for Obama's pragmatist aspirations. Dissenters might still be valuable participants in our democratic life. They may not have turned away from America; they may instead be holding fast to a richer and more expansive vision of it. If one must accept a triumphalist vision of the civil rights struggle in order to be a party to ongoing deliberations about how to extend, consolidate, or restore the gains of that struggle, if, in other words, arguing that the vision is incomplete marks one as having turned away from the shared democratic project, then what becomes of the pragmatic aspiration to open-ended and shared democratic inquiry? What happens to, as we saw Hayes put it earlier, refusing the "certainties derived from abstractions," including abstractions like "America" or, better, "anti-American"?

We can bring this line of thinking to a close by reflecting on Mr. Obama's best-known attempt at post-racial civic identity-construction: his Philadelphia race speech. To his credit, the speech is a rhetorical marvel, and a model of concise but responsible reflection on complex historical and ethical issues. It offers a remarkable short course on the systematic production of racial inequality over time. It successfully argues that people with different views on racial politics—reduced, for ease of exposition I'm sure, largely to two sides, one black and one white—have concerns that can't be wished away. And it makes clear, in line with the best theories of democratic deliberation and communication, that progress will be impossible until each side begins by crediting the other side's perspective.

But consider the occasion of the speech, and the way Mr. Obama dealt with it. He came to Philadelphia to quell the controversy that arose when the public caught wind of inflammatory speeches by Jeremiah Wright, the pastor of his former church in Chicago. Mr. Wright was harshly critical of America as such, saying in one place that "God bless America" rings less true than "God damn America," in light of the way the US comports itself in the world. Then-Senator Obama had to distance himself from this language on pain of losing any hope of broad electoral success; but he had to do it in a way that did not reawaken fears that he was "not black enough," on pain of losing what would soon be the most natural and reliable portion of his base.

After wonderfully humanizing his former pastor, rescuing him from the raving lunatic that had taken his place in the imaginations and conversations of cable news pundits, Mr. Obama points out that Rev. Wright "came of age . . . [at] a time when segregation was still the law of the land and opportunity was systematically constricted." For people of this generation, he continues, "the memories of humiliation and doubt and fear have not gone away; nor has the anger and the bitterness. . . ." Unfortunately, "[t]hat anger is not always productive; indeed, all too often it distracts attention from solving real problems." This, it turns out, was Wright's mistake, in a way: "The profound mistake of Reverend Wright's sermons is not that he spoke about racism in our society. It's that he spoke as if our society was static; as if no progress has been made."[29]

As I've noted, the speech is in many ways a remarkable achievement. But it is remarkable in part for the subtlety of its post-racial and—more to the point right now—counter-pragmatic evasions. In the span of a few short paragraphs, a sophisticated critique of racial inequality gets reduced to a contest of resentments between angry blacks and bitter whites. As a result, grievances— ways of registering conditions in need of change—become mere feelings, which changes them from problems to be solved into sensibilities or perceptions to be managed.

Similarly, the complicated conditions that fueled Wright's anger fall away, taking with them the possibility that Wright had a valid critique, and that, if the critique is valid, anger might be an appropriate accompaniment. And as these go, so goes the possibility that Wright can see, like any sensible person, that things have changed, but that, as racial formation theory counsels us to say, this change might not constitute progress—and that this thought might have some bearing on the shared deliberations that inform our democratic culture. We know from James Baldwin and many others that vigorous criticism of America is not the same thing as refusal or repudiation. Wright has seen change, remains critical, but also remains here—and, as Mr. Obama points out, served in the military. Perhaps people who share his views have something to tell us about what America is now; they needn't simply be stuck in a time warp, locked into the prejudices and resentments of the Moses generation.

Could Mr. Obama have given any credence to this more complicated reading of Rev. Wright and retained any hope of winning the presidency? Probably not, unless he had an even better speech in him than the rather remarkable one he gave. But again, this might just go to a deeper point about the Obama-as-pragmatist line. Perhaps it is impossible for someone to aspire responsibly to the presidency while also holding fast to pragmatic commitments. This raises a question for another time—the question of what the presidency is, and of what the US is now, and of whether they are what we want them to be, or what they can be. The question we can consider right now is narrower, and one we have in fact already introduced. Do repressed pragmatic commitments remain operative somewhere, somewhere deep down? Or does the willingness to set them aside—as it were, pragmatically—actually mean that the commitments are not operative at all?

QUESTIONING THE QUESTION; OR, INQUIRY AND DESIRE

Obama the writer, the presidential candidate, and the campaign orator looks much more like a pragmatist than Obama the president does. And we can insist that the earlier Obama control our reading of the later one only by arbitrarily confining him, confining our sense of who and what this man is, to a particular moment in his personal growth, or by dubiously insisting on some pragmatic essence that somehow hides beneath or underwrites his every action. Neither move seems appropriate to anyone who takes pragmatism seriously.

It would be odd if an affirmative answer to the question of Obama's pragmatism forced us to turn his pragmatism into a matter of an unmanifested essence, mired somewhere deep inside of him. But it might be worth asking what it means to ask the question, and to expect only affirmative or negative responses. Instead of accepting that "he is" and "he isn't" are the only proper replies, perhaps we should do what Peirce does, early on, to Descartes' methodological doubt, or what Dewey does, in his better moments, to the problem of the external world. We should, in other words, decline to assume that the question has earned its claim on our attention. We might instead ask: Why is *that* the question? And: What does it say about us that *this* is what we puzzle over?

On one level, the matter is perfectly straightforward. A powerful public figure makes the kind of noises that we've come to expect, recently, at least, only from professional philosophers of a certain sort. What's more, he does this in a country that is perpetually haunted by rabid anti-intellectualism, and that is currently shadowed by severe skepticism about the life of the mind and about the industry and enterprise that traditionally supports this life—the higher education sector. Given that context, it makes sense that we'd want to examine the depth of the president's commitment to this philosophical orientation. In addition, there's the matter, noted above, of the need for some help in divining the meaning of this unfamiliar president. If he makes pragmatic noises and marks, and if reading him in light of these leads to a more plausible, more interesting, and more accurate picture of the man, then we *should* be drawn to the question of his pragmatism.

On another level, though, the issue may be more complicated, in a way that requires a shift from argument to diagnosis. And perhaps this in turn requires a shift in tone, in the direction of greater diffidence and of words like "perhaps" and expressions like "I wonder." So: Perhaps the thought of Mr. Obama as a pragmatist reassures us, some of us, that the president is some kind of political heir to Deweyan progressivism (whatever one thinks Dewey is), and allows us to ignore the mounting evidence—mounting, some would say, since well before 2008, and present from the beginning in Mr. Obama's own freely announced fondness for centrism—that he is anything but. Or, for those who are not drawn to Dewey's politics, call this "guild socialism" or "renascent liberalism" if "progressivism" will not do: I wonder if the thought of Obama's pragmatism appeals because it makes the president an oasis in a sea of anti-intellectualism. It makes him a philosopher, and reminds us that he was once an academic, and it does this just as the professional practices of philosophy and of humanistic inquiry are increasingly threatened with disrespect, irrelevance, and defunding, along with the higher education sector as a whole.

These possibilities and others like them are worth a moment of reflection because they mark the question of Mr. Obama's pragmatism as an expression of desire. They mark it, in other words, as an occasion for heightened self-scrutiny, for cultivating the discipline to distinguish the world we want to see from the world that is actually in the making. This is not an abstract point about the mechanisms and arts of subject formation as such, or it is not just that. It is also, and I hope mainly, a point about the work anyone must do if they aspire properly to the condition, to bear up under the burdens and realize the opportunities, of social intelligence and democratic citizenship.

CONCLUSION

This discussion began with an assumption that I've maintained throughout, but that by now we might want to revisit. The thought was that the way to cash out Mr. Obama's self-professed aspirations to post-partisanship was by reading them through his also self-professed fondness for some kind of pragmatism, and by then reading that through specifically philosophical pragmatism. But what if this is wrong? What if post-partisanship is not about pragmatism at all?

A deeper, more vigorous critique of the president might begin here. We've reached the end of this discussion, so I'll turn once more to gestures. Perhaps what appears to be post-partisanship is really an advanced form of bipartisanship. Perhaps what really unifies Mr. Obama's political persona is his acceptance of certain commitments that also unite the two major parties in the US. Some of these commitments have to do with the boundaries of legitimate discourse, which exclude alternative party formations like the Greens and the Libertarians. Some have to do with the centrality of the financial services industry to our politics and our economy, and of the military and surveillance apparatuses to the operation of the state. And some have to do with the need to proliferate market transactions across multiple domains of human experience and encounter, and, accordingly, to privilege our identities as consumers over our identities as citizens.

This might be a more fruitful direction for exploring the idea of contemporary post-partisanship. This is not the place to light out in that direction. But clearing away the thought of the president as a pragmatist—whatever we end up saying about Mr. Obama the writer, or otherwise in his heart of hearts—may help clarify the value of this other exploration when its time comes.

NOTES

1 Barack Obama, "Democratic National Convention Keynote Address," wash ingtonpost.com, posted July 27, 2004, accessed November 27, 2014 at www. washingtonpost.com/wp-dyn/articles/A19751-2004Jul27.html

2 Ibid.

3 Gary Wills, "Behind Obama's Cool," *The New York Times*, April 7, 2010, accessed August 20, 2012 at www.nytimes.com/2010/04/11/books/review/Wills-t.html?pagewanted=all&_r=0

4 Chris Hayes, "The Pragmatist," *The Nation*, posted December 10, 2008 (print version, 29 December), par. 1; accessed February 19, 2010 at www.thenation. com/doc/20081229/hayes

5 Sam Youngman, "Democratic Party unrest plays out in Emanuel controversy," *The Hill*, March 7, 2010, par. 3; accessed November 27, 2014 at http://thehill. com/homenews/administration/85353-unrest-in-democratic-party-plays-out-in-emanuel-controversy

6 Hayes, par. 5.

7 Hayes, par. 13.

8 Hayes, par. 18.

9 Charles Sanders Peirce, "The Fixation of Belief," *Popular Science Monthly* 12 (1877), 1–15; *The Collected Papers of Charles Sanders Peirce, Electronic Edition, Volume 5: Pragmatism and Pragmaticism*, Charles Hartshorne and Paul Weiss, Eds. (Charlottesville, Virginia: InteLex, 1994) §386.

10 Hayes, par. 22.

11 Robert Talisse, *A Pragmatist Philosophy of Democracy* (New York: Routledge, 2007), 66.

12 Bart Schultz, "Obama's Political Philosophy: Pragmatism, Politics, and the University of Chicago," *Philosophy of the Social Sciences* 39 (2009), 127–173, 134; accessed February 19, 2010 at http://pos.sagepub.com/content/39/2/127

13 Schultz, 2009, 134.

14 Hayes, par. 2.

15 Schultz, 2009, 155, citing *Audacity* 97–98.

16 Schultz, 2009, 161.

17 Schultz, 2009, 160.

18 Schultz, 2009, 136.

19 Eldridge, Michael, "Barack Obama's Pragmatism," www.obamaspragmatism. info/, Website initially posted March 21, 2009; last updated August 9, 2009; accessed December 9, 2010.

20 Lawson, Bill and Donald Koch, Eds., *Pragmatism and the Problem of Race* (Bloomington, IN: Indiana University Press, 2004), 139.

21 Obama, Barack, "Remarks By the President In Health Insurance Reform Town Hall," August 11, 2009, accessed September 15, 2011 at www.whitehouse.gov/the_press_office/Remarks-by-the-President-at-Town-Hall-on-Health-Insurance-Reform-in-Portsmouth-New-Hampshire/

22 Wallsten, Peter. "Chief of Staff Draws Fire from Left as Obama Falters." *Wall Street Journal*, January 26, 2010, Eastern edition, accessed November 29, 2014 at http://search.proquest.com/docview/399092669?accountid=13158

23 Micah Sifry, "The Obama Disconnect: What Happens When Myth Meets Reality," *Techpresident* blog, at Personal Democracy Media, posted December 31, 2009, available at http://techpresident.com/blog-entry/the-obama-disconnect; accessed November 28, 2014; citing David Plouffe, *The Audacity To Win* (New York: Penguin, 2010), 372.

24 "Recently Revealed 'Secrecy Pact' for Trans-Pacific Trade Talks Belies Obama Administration Promises of Transparency in Trade," Press Release, Public Citizen (Washington DC.), October 18, 2011; accessed November 28, 2014 at www.citizen.org/release-the-text-letters

25 Jack Serle, "More than 2,400 dead as Obama's drone campaign marks five years," *The Bureau of Investigative Journalism*, January 23, 2014, accessed November 28, 2014 at www.thebureauinvestigates.com/2014/01/23/more-than-2400-dead-as-obamas-drone-campaign-marks-five-years/

26 DeYoung, Karen and Greg Miller. "U.S. Curbs Drone Strikes in Pakistan, Officials Say." *News India—Times*, February 14, 2014, accessed November 29,

2014 at http://search.proquest.com/docview/1510220679?accountid=13158; originally published at *Washingtonpost.com* on February 4, 2014, available at www.washingtonpost.com/world/national-security/us-curtails-drone-strikes-in-pakistan-as-officials-there-seek-peace-talks-with-taliban/2014/02/04/1d63f52a-8dd8-11e3-833c-33098f9e5267_story.html

27 Leo Strauss, a twentieth-century historian of philosophy and political philosopher, "argued that, when reading certain pre-modern thinkers, it is necessary to read between the lines. The possibility of persecution gives rise to a certain type of writing that allows one set of the readers, the majority, to receive one message while allowing a second set of readers, the philosophical elite, to take away another message. . . . [T]he most persistent and serious misunderstanding of Strauss is that he promotes mass deception. On this reading, Strauss suggests that the masses simply cannot handle the truth and are in need of a class of political elites who, while themselves pursuing the truth, support the noble lies necessary for any society to function." Leora Batnitzky, "Leo Strauss", Edward N. Zalta, Ed., *The Stanford Encyclopedia of Philosophy* (Winter 2010 Edition), par. 10 and 61, accessed November 29, 2014 at http://plato.stanford.edu/archives/win2010/entries/strauss-leo/

28 John Dewey, Reconstruction in Philosophy—The Middle Works of John Dewey, 1899–1924, Vol. 12 (1920; Charlottesville, VA: InteLex, 2003), 128.

29 Obama, "A More Perfect Union", 242, 244, 245.

Three

Moses agreed to stay with the man, and he gave Moses his daughter Zipporah in marriage. She bore a son, and he named him Gershom; for he said, "I have been an alien residing in a foreign land."

(Exodus 2:21–22, New Revised Version)

. . . Zipporah took a flint and cut off her son's foreskin, and touched Moses' feet with it, and said, "Truly you are a bridegroom of blood to me!"

(Exodus 4:25, New Revised Version)

INAUGURATION DAYDREAMS

I happened to be staying in a hotel on the day of Barack Obama's first inauguration. People gathered to watch the proceedings in the hotel bar. They peered up at the wall-mounted television in rapt attention. Aretha Franklin sang. The people in the bar cheered.

The excitement that filled the bar also dominated the newscast. A stream of text messages from delighted viewers ran on a ticker at the bottom of the screen. It conveyed the same elated, over-the-top messages that the news anchors occasionally stirred themselves to deliver. At any moment in the broadcast, a viewer had a very good chance to hear or see someone say, "this is the realization of Dr. King's dream," or "we are seeing the resuscitation of the American dream."

The camera eventually cut away from the newsreaders to show crowds of joyous black people celebrating in the streets of the nation's capital. I should say, we saw this scene in *one of* the nation's capitals, because this nation has three. The parliament sits in Cape Town, the executive's offices are in Pretoria, and the supreme court of appeal sits in Bloemfontein.

GLOBAL POLITICS AFTER HISTORY

I watched Mr. Obama's inauguration in South Africa, in an out-of-the-way place called "Hogsback." Judging by the enthusiasm that gripped the country, though, I could as well have been in Baltimore or Atlanta. The difference is that few residents of those quint-essentially American "chocolate cities" would have been likely to express their enthusiasm in quite the way the South Africans did. One contribution to the SABC ticker feed tells the tale. "He," the viewer wrote, referring to the USA's newly minted president, "is the world's Moses."

The thought of Mr. Obama as Moses, and, more than this, as *the world's* Moses, points to the final mode of post-historicism that I want to explore in this book. (In light of our earlier reflections on the president's discussions of the Joshua generation, it also points to another respect in which he is something of a chameleon, or a blank screen. He can be both Joshua *and* Moses, albeit for different audiences.) The 44th president was seen as a healer and uniter, and as a balm for the untreated wounds of ethnoracial injustice, not just on the domestic front, but also around the world. He spoke before massive and adoring crowds in Europe even before his election, in an odd international star turn that famously culminated at Germany's Brandenburg Gate. The prospect of his election led reporters to visit Kenya and Indonesia, where they sought and always found excited anticipation among ordinary people in the candidate's old and ancestral homelands. Newspapers in Amsterdam ran headlines like this: "With Obama, cynicism is past."[1]

Some of this enthusiasm of course had to do with Mr. Obama's predecessor. George W. Bush was widely disliked, even more outside the US than within. And he was widely regarded as dangerously bellicose, either impulsive or corrupt (depending on how one explained the bellicosity), and indifferent to the prospects for and requirements of global cooperation and comity.

But the world's openness to Mr. Obama, the global fascination with him and hunger for him, went beyond his status as an alternative to President Bush. For many people, he seemed to represent the same kind of historical break that we've seen in the previous chapters. Where before we were supposed to leave behind race-thinking or partisan ideologies, what we leave behind here is a kind of imperial hubris.

In this celebration of American *glasnost*, we see the president's post-historical aura put in the first of four standard relationships to the ideas of empire and of the nation. Each of these relationships reflects in its own way the impulse to historical transcendence in the context of global affairs. And each yields a distinctive mode of post-historical global politics.

The first mode—we can think of this as an anti-imperial or positive post-colonial mode—reads the rise of the Obamas as evidence that the US has finally accepted the end of "the American century," and is prepared to work with its global partners instead of dictating to them. On this approach, Obama's new world will be safer than Bush's, shaped less by hierarchy and relations of domination than by cooperation and partnership. And it will be this way in part because one of the clearest occasions for hierarchy, a constellation of assumptions about differential racial capacities and worth, has clearly been repudiated. As one of the ticker writers put it, "a son of Africa" was now the most powerful man in the world, and that made all the difference.

A second mode—think of this as an *anti-anti-imperialist mode*—begins just where celebratory anti-imperialism does, with the idea that America is stepping back from its familiar, outsize global role; but it sees this not as progress but as a misstep. According to this approach, the new limits on American power have been to some degree put there by Americans who should know better, and should be scolded and resisted rather than applauded.

The third mode of global post-historicism—we can think of this as a *neo-imperial or negative post-colonial* mode—also saw

Mr. Obama's election as a marker of decline. The issue here, though, is not a retreat from the commanding heights of American soft and hard power, but a detour on the journey away from colonial domination and exploitation. On this approach, Mr. Obama belongs to the familiar class of "elite anti-colonial leaders" on whose watch "liberatory gains are turned back."[2]

The final mode of global post-historicism—think of this as a *post-national* mode—sees the Obama administration as the consummation or cessation of certain globalizing tendencies in American and world politics. The key idea here is that with Mr. Obama we see the intensification of various forces that establish global elites beyond the authority and reach of traditional nation-states. The best real-world emblem for this phenomenon may be the World Trade Organization (WTO), or any of the multilateral trade agreements that have been proposed in the wake of the North American Free Trade Agreement (NAFTA).

The burden of this chapter, as in the previous chapters, is to think through the warrant for and implications of seeing Mr. Obama as a post-historical figure, but this time in relation to ideas like "empire." I'll try in what follows to distinguish between the instructive and the distracting ways of thinking of Mr. Obama as a post-imperial figure, on the assumption that even the troubling versions of this thought track something that is worth our attention. As in the previous chapters, these thoughts will appear in a variety of places, from newspapers to scholarly articles; and as before, it may turn out that what these thoughts track is the progress of certain desires and aversions.

The previous chapters have begun to show that post-historicism has less to do with what Mr. Obama is than with what other people want or need him to be, and with his remarkable ability, as he himself noted, to become a blank screen onto which people project their wants and needs.[3] Tracking these projections in the spheres of geopolitics and international relations will bring more fully into focus some dynamics that have figured in the previous arguments, like the bait and switch of post-racial liberatory politics. But it will also raise for consideration some issues that have not yet figured prominently in the discussion, especially as these coalesce around

Michelle Obama—the Zipporah to Mr. Obama's Moses—and around the cultural institutions of the presidency and the First Family.

There are many ways to approach the questions about global politics that bear on the topic of this chapter. One way requires thinking with care, in light of detailed empirical information, about just where the United States stands in world affairs these days, and about the efficacy of its recent exercises in foreign policy. Committing fully to this approach would require detailed studies in international relations and policy analysis that I can't undertake here. At most, I will rely here and there on fairly accessible and general information about US politics and global affairs. I will instead focus more on the unexpected ways in which conceptions of things like empires register in public culture. Committing fully to this alternative approach would also mean encroaching on the turf of other fields, fields like intellectual history and literary theory. My hope is to find an intermediate space, somewhere between Gayatri Spivak and the World Bank, for coherent and accessible philosophical reflection on the thought of a post-imperial US presidency.

ON IMPERIALISM, AND OTHER CONCEPTS

As a first step toward thinking of Mr. Obama as a post-imperial figure in any of the modes indicated above, it is important to clarify the conceptual environment that sustains these modes of thinking. The most obvious concepts to wrestle with are "imperialism" and related notions like "colonialism." But first, because it will go more quickly, we'll need to consider what it means to talk about states, about nations, and about the nation some people call "America."

NATIONS, STATES, AND NATIONALISM

A state is a particular way of organizing a political community. It is, specifically, that mode of political organization in which some people have authority over others, which is to say that some have the right to be obeyed by the others. It is also, some people think, to say that this right carries with it the further right, and the exclusive right, to use force to compel compliance, though students of international law, at least, think of the monopoly of coercive force as inessential. Either way, the state's authority is vested in some kind of governmental apparatus, distinct from other social institutions; and both the governors and their subjects are members of a permanent population and inhabit a defined territory.[4]

The rise of European modernity brought with it, and was in part defined by, a new form of the state, with new additions to the basic formula. The governmental apparatus became increasingly bureaucratized, statecraft became increasingly bound up with management and with gathering information (which is where the idea of "statistics" comes from—from the state's need to collect facts about its domain). At the same time, territorial boundaries became more precise, and standing armies and the techniques of total war were (eventually) brought to bear on, among other things, protecting those boundaries. All of this interacted in different ways in different places with distinctively modern ideas about what political authority looked like and when this authority was legitimate, as well as with modern ideas about gender roles and economic life. Ideas about individual freedom, democracy, property, and markets, ideas that we now take for granted, came to be part of the field on which states operated.

Nationalism is a distinctive way of distilling a set of political commitments and ideologies from the normative structure of the modern state. Nationalism in the wild, as it were, takes many forms, like any ideology. But its ideal type has at least five features. For the ideal-typical nationalist, citizens ought to be in solidarity with each other, united in bonds of fellow-feeling beyond simply sharing territory. Citizens should also feel loyalty to the political community, rather than simply obeying its commands as a condition of enjoying certain benefits. The community that the citizens constitute is usually supposed to present itself as an organic, functionally homogenous unit, with multiple aspects of its life, from its literature and language to its marriage rites and orientation to the martial virtues, all expressing a common sensibility or essence. This constellation of practices and sensibilities is supposed to be unique, interestingly unlike the combinations of attributes that define other nations. And the uniqueness of this community requires sovereignty—the space and power to express the nation's distinctive way of life without hindrance, for example, in a sovereign state.[5]

The fact of the modern state and the ideology of nationalism come together in an instructive way in the idea of America. The United States of America is a geopolitical unit, with relations to other states and particular bureaucratic and institutional structures. But *America* is something over and above this political reality. "America" refers to the collection of narratives, images, myths, and symbols that, for many people, the United States should organize itself to defend and express. America in this sense is an exceptional place, defined by its world-historical commitment to freedom and equality, by its openness to immigrants, by the practical bent—in commerce and technology, above all—of its people: by, in short, its open embrace and clear manifestation of the modern age. The gap between the reality of the US and the idea of America is what people are insisting on when they point out that South America is America too, and that the place that aspired to be a new birth of freedom, as Lincoln put it at Gettysburg, needed a new birth because the original one enshrined slavery at the heart of the national enterprise. And the appeal of this idea is what people register when they declare, for example, that torturing terror suspects is not what America is about, which is to say, depending on the speaker, either that it therefore didn't happen, and *couldn't have* happened, or that the people who did it should be punished. It is also, in the alternative, what other people register when they say that America is the world's best hope for freedom, or justice, or order, and that whatever we do is therefore right.

The sketch of states, nations, and nationalism offered above flirts with a thought that I'll now need to make explicit: modern states, along with other markers of modernity like capitalism and democracy (as we know it), emerged from and defined a broad social formation that also had race-thinking at its core. Nationalism became a going concern in part because ideas of racial difference were taking shape as well. That is: it gets easier to think of a political community as a unique organic whole, expressing its shared life in every one of its members and aspects, when the idea of race is available to give content to the national spirit or essence.

The collision and convergence of these modern conditions produced yet another defining feature of European modernity: imperial expansion. The world had long had empires of various kinds. But scientific and technological breakthroughs—in weaponry and shipbuilding, among other things—combined with new economic imperatives and new ideas about the differential worth of various human types to produce the novel phenomenon of racialized transoceanic empires, as epitomized by the French and the British. This innovation brings us a step closer to the real work of this chapter: thinking through the claim that the Obama presidency has in some sense been a post-imperial phenomenon. Taking the next step requires a clearer understanding of what modern imperialism involves.

EMPIRES AND COLONIES

The idea of empire is a familiar one, but one that it will still pay us to define with some care. We can say with Jennifer Pitts that an empire is a "large and expansionist" polity that reproduces "differentiation and inequality among people it incorporates" or annexes.[6] People often freely toggle back and forth between the concepts of imperialism and colonialism as if they are interchangeable, but strictly speaking, which is to say, in terms of the logic of the concepts, an imperial polity is not necessarily a colonialist enterprise. After all, a state needn't manifest its imperial ambitions by planting colonies—that is, exporting its own citizens to set up shop—in foreign lands. If imperialism involves, as theologian Reinhold Niebuhr puts it, the "problem of using power in global terms," of how and whether "to dominate [others] by our power," then there are surely ways to do that without planting colonies.[7] Expansion, incorporation, and annexation might simply involve bringing more and more of the world into the polity's sphere of dominating influence—think here of the Monroe Doctrine, or the Roosevelt Corollary, or, perhaps, of NAFTA (as its critics understand it, in any case).

While it is not conceptually necessary for an empire to be colonialist, the actual political and cultural contexts for modern empires have nevertheless forged a tight relationship between these modes of political organization. The great modern empires— I'll join Edward Said in focusing on the French and British empires, for reasons like his[8]—were vigorous and massive colonial enterprises. The British Empire at its height, just after World War I, covered a quarter of the globe, and its French counterpart controlled another one-tenth.[9] These sprawling enterprises enabled massive resource transfers from subject lands to colonial metropoles, and shaped, and continue to shape, the prospects, cultures, and experiences of enormous numbers of people, as surely as their need for resources and markets shaped the economies and the literal spatial configurations of the countries these people inhabit.

Colonialism insinuated itself into the workings of modern imperialism, and consequently into the workings of the modern world, in part by providing a store of resources for imagining and conceiving of the participants in Europe's imperial dramas. As Said points out, "'imperialism' means the practice, the theory, and *the attitudes* of a dominating metropolitan center ruling a distant territory."[10] He continues: "imperialism . . . lingers where it has always been, in a kind of general cultural sphere as well as in specific political, ideological, economic, and social practices. . . . [It is] supported and . . . impelled by impressive ideological formations [according to which] certain territories and people *require* and beseech domination. . . ."[11]

Imperialism's ideological formations were shaped by colonial encounters with "exotic" peoples in "alien" lands, encounters that informed and were informed by emerging conceptions of specifically racial difference. Modern empires were racial projects, in the sense of that expression discussed in Chapter 1. They appealed to racialized understandings of human difference and capacity to "reproduce differentiation and inequality" on a colossal scale.

These empires were not just racial projects, of course, in part because racial projects are never just racial projects, but also because of the considerations that accounts of intersectionality mean for us to keep in mind.[12] It has not been inconsequential to the modern practice of imperialism that these empires thought of themselves as civilizing missions, bringing the light of reason and such things to the backward, darker races. But it is also not inconsequential that the backwardness of these races was supposed to be evident in part from their ways of organizing, or of failing to organize, gender and sexuality; or that ceasing to be backward was supposed to mean embracing north Atlantic conceptions not just of sexual propriety and gender identity, but also of economic and wider cultural life.

Put differently: Colonialism may not be internal to the concept of imperialism, but the phenomenon of imperialism in the modern world has in fact been intimately bound up with the more or less familiar clusters of practices and sensibilities that gives our modern empires their distinctive characters. These clusters pair discursive and ideological structures with colonialism's formal economic and political structures, with the result that certain habits of perception, expression, and attention—what Said calls "structures of attitude and reference"[13]—get sunk deep into the roots of the colonized and colonizing societies. Said's structures largely survive the official dismantling of the political arrangements between colonizer and colonized, and come—along with persistent arrangements in political economy that they help sustain—to define what I will call "coloniality."

ON COLONIALITY

I'll have more to say in the sections to come about the content of our colonial structures, both discursive and material. For now some gestures will have to suffice. The first gesture will concern material structures, and provide a glimpse of the economic and human consequences of imperial modes of social organization. The remaining gestures will concern discursive structures, and begin to tease out the political implications of Said's structures of attitude and reference.

We might appeal to any number of statistical or historical considerations in order to lay bare the redistributive project at the heart of modern imperialism. Consider for example that "[b]etween 1905 and 1914, 50 percent of Dahomey's gross domestic product (GDP) was extracted by the French."[14] Or that, as freely reported by contemporaneous analysts, Britain's profits from colonial trade, either directly in slaves or in industries powered by slave labor, "provided . . . the capital which financed the industrial revolution."[15] Or, shifting from economic to human costs, consider that during the colonial era,

> [i]n North America and Brazil the relatively small indigenous population was marginalized or exterminated, in former Spanish colonies the indigenous population remained as an underclass, and in all the areas where slavery was important their descendants have also remained an underprivileged group.[16]

The most vivid emblem of this redistributive project, though, may be the remarkable story of the Belgian Congo. At the turn of the twentieth century, King Leopold of Belgium established a personal fiefdom in central Africa, and extracted labor and resources from it with astonishing brutality. Eventually the viciousness of his reign turned global opinion against him even in the age of empire, and this, combined with geopolitical pressures, persuaded him to transfer the territory to the Belgian state. The tally from his reign was staggering: the Belgian government assumed 110 million francs in Leopold's debts, paid 45 million francs more toward the completion of various projects, and gave the king 50 million francs in installment payments—to be taken from the proceeds of the colony's continued operations.[17] (One Belgian franc was probably worth about $5US at the time, which might be around $100 in 2013 dollars, based on the change in the purchaser price index. So each of Leopold's millions was worth around $100M today.)[18] The human toll of Leopold's violent reign—as depicted in Conrad's *Heart of Darkness* and reprised in Coppola's "Apocalypse Now"—

is comparably striking. There are too many accounts of mutilation and brutality, of limbs severed to punish lassitude and villages razed to discourage dissent, to recount here. But there is also, again, the tally: between 1880 and 1920, the population of the Congo region appears to have shrunk by about half—some ten million people.[19]

The second gesture at the structures of imperialism comes from Francophone studies scholar Dominic Thomas, and begins with a comment about France that could apply, *mutatis mutandis*, to any former colonial power. Thomas writes, "the specter of French colonial history continues to haunt the national psyche, inserting itself into concerns pertaining to diversity and multiculturalism, identity, education, religious tolerance, and of course immigration policy."[20] What does this haunting look like? We can find a response in Thomas' reference to a Nicolas Sarkozy speech from 2007, delivered shortly after Sarkozy won the French presidency:

> The tragedy of Africa is that the African has not fully entered into history. The African peasant, who for thousands of years has lived according to the seasons and whose life ideal has been to live harmoniously with nature, has only ever known the eternal renewal of time, punctuated by the endless repetition of the same gestures and the same words. In this imaginary world where everything starts over and over again there is no place for human adventure or for the idea of progress.[21]

Commentators of all sorts pilloried Sarkozy for rehearsing what the chairman of the African Union Commission referred to as "declarations of a bygone era."[22] Developing this complaint further would require showing just how these obsolete, weirdly Hegelian declarations fail to capture the complexity of African life. There are many ways to do this, from a genealogical critique of the pernicious idea of "traditional society" to an empirical survey of the long, pre-encounter history of urbanism and complex social organization in what we now call "Africa." And something like this move is essential, in order to complicate the facile claim that, its brutality and theft notwithstanding, imperialism did in fact bring civilization to the natives. But following these moves out any farther—any farther than I will, right now, by stipulating to my reliance on them—would exceed the mandate of this project. The point right now is just that the colonialist's "bygone era" continued to declare itself in—to haunt—Sarkozy's policies, and continues to do the same for politics, policy, and social life well beyond Paris.

CULLWICK, MUNBY, AND COLONIAL IDENTITIES

The third gesture comes from Anne McClintock's discussion of a notorious—among social historians and literary theorists, anyway—cultural expression of colonialist attitudinal structures. This last gesture is important because Sarkozy's account of dark people living timelessly in the state of nature gives voice to just some of our familiar colonial attitudes. His account leads naturally into certain other familiar ideas, like the conception of empty, unimproved land (because, remember, there is no progress in the state of nature), a conception that John Locke enshrined in his references to *terra nullius* and that so clearly underwrote European settlement in North America, South Africa, and Australia. But it refers at best obliquely to the intersectional nature of coloniality. The colonial project was not just about race, but was vitally about the co-constitution of simultaneously racialized, gendered, and economic subjects. As McClintock puts it, "imperialism cannot be fully understood without a theory of gender power" because "gender dynamics were, from the outset, fundamental to the . . . imperial enterprise."[23]

After reminding her readers that Europeans routinely depicted their explorers, with varying degrees of explicitness, as engaged in masculine quests to conquer virgin territories, McClintock uses the story of white Britons Hannah Cullwick and Arthur Munby to exemplify the articulation of race with gender and class in the construction of colonial identities. The story begins like this:

In May 1854, at the age of 25, Arthur Munby stopped a maid of-all-work in the street [in London]. . . . Almost immediately, Hannah Cullwick and Arthur Munby embarked on an intense but clandestine love affair that lasted the rest of their lives. After nineteen years, they married secretly, though they lived in the same house for only four years and then, to all appearances, only as master and housemaid.[24]

Cullwick and Munby hid their relationship from public view because their intimacies were built around a peculiar performance, or set of performances, of Victorian identities. A reviewer for one of the several books about the pair—all drawing heavily on the many writings and photographs that the two meticulously composed, exchanged, and left behind—puts it this way:

Cullwick . . . came to spend 40 years in a sado-masochistic relationship where her greatest treat was to be allowed to lick her husband's dirty boots (horse shit was her favourite relish). Cullwick's private name for Munby was "massa", an uneasy term that looked back to her native Shropshire dialect and elided it with that of the negro slave whose blackness she replicated with soot, as much for her own pleasure as for his. Packed into those two syllables were all the social, sexual and racial inflections that made their connection so forbidden and so binding.[25]

The reviewer sees the Cullwick-Munby relationship as a window onto the peculiarity of Victorian sexual practices, with social, sexual, and racial "inflections." But McClintock sees it also, I think rightly, as a highly condensed and perspicuous manifestation of colonial attitudes, with abiding conceptions of human difference at its core.

Cullwick and Munby were clearly fascinated by the class politics that framed their relationship, but just as clearly, even ostentatiously, explored other dimensions of social differentiation as well. Cullwick continued to work as a maid despite Munby's securely middle-class status as a barrister, and the couple enacted elaborate public and private ruses to maintain and play on their occupational and status differences. Munby would, for example, patronize establishments where Cullwick worked, where she would serve him as just another of the patrons until they could steal away to be alone. They would also play out nanny–infant scenarios, with Cullwick cradling Munby in her arms—which had apparently, and to Munby's delight, become remarkably strong from years of menial labor—like a baby. There's more:

> [Cullwick] posed for numerous photographs: as her working self in "her dirt"; crossdressed as an upper-class lady; as a rural maiden, a man, an angel, a male slave, and "almost nude" and blackened from head to foot as a male chimney-sweep. When they married secretly after nineteen years, she cross-dressed as an upper-middle class lady and traveled with Munby around Europe. Back in London, she would arrange to theatrically scrub the front doorsteps on her knees as Munby sauntered down the street, languidly swinging his cane.[26]

McClintock sees in this relationship, in its fetishisms and sado-masochistic tendencies, the intersectional convergence of meanings that modern imperialism created, relied on, and sustained. Linking colonial meanings and Victorian identities is the sort of move that, once it gets made, seems obvious. But modern racialism's determination to hide its workings from view, to depict them as natural and inevitable, makes the move easy to overlook. The Victorian era overlapped with the high point of British imperialism, which made colonial attitudes grist for the mill of Victorian identity construction and sexual play. This matters for us now because these same attitudes continue to inform—to haunt—the way we imagine and pursue our prospects today.

The Cullwick–Munby story functions here as a case study in the convergence of meanings that helps define modern coloniality. It serves first of all to excavate this convergence and bring it into view. But McClintock explains the deeper point:

The primary transformations about which their fantasy games revolved were the central transformations of industrial imperialism: class (servant to mistress), race (white woman to black slave), gender (woman to man), economy (land to city) and age (adult to baby), transformations that were drawn simultaneously from the cult of domesticity and the cult of empire.[27]

This is no doubt an extreme case, but the best ones often are, as readers raised on twin-earth and brain-in-vat thought experiments might attest. More to the point, the case may seem at best distantly related to the post-imperial aspirations of the Obama presidency. The sections to come should correct for this, but, unfortunately, not right away. Now that the convergence is on the table—now that we've aired the thought that imperialism is partly about coloniality, and that coloniality is bound up with the co-constitution of racial, gendered, and economic identities—I'll have to set it aside. It will take a little time, and some more work, to get to the point at which the intersectional nature of coloniality can function productively in an argument about the Obama presidency.

THE POST-HISTORICAL PRESIDENCY: FOUR READINGS

With that lengthy but necessary detour through some key concepts complete, it is finally time to relate these considerations to the Obama presidency. Mr. Obama's post-historical possibilities interested students of global affairs in four basic ways, all relating in some way to the thought that the "American century" has ended. Two of these approaches, referred to above as anti-imperialist and anti-anti-imperialist, see American imperial aspirations chastened, and either applaud or object. Two other approaches, referred to above as neo-imperialist and post-national, accept that the world has changed but insist that empire remains, altered but persistent, and perhaps resurgent.

All four of these approaches begin with the same assumption— that American power, at least as we have traditionally understood it, is in decline. But what, exactly, does this mean? And why would anyone think this? The post-imperialist readings to come will develop this assumption to some degree, but it may help to set the stage in advance.

The basic point is simple enough: as political scientist Adam Quinn puts it in a piece we'll soon revisit, "the United States is in decline in the sense that its power, measured in resources and resultant capacity to disproportionately affect others, is, and will in future be . . . significantly less than it has been."[28] Quinn goes on to point out that this decline may be a function of two perhaps complementary processes. The US might be growing weaker internally, as it might be, due to the stresses on the economy. In addition, other nations and powers, like India, Brazil, China, and Russia, might be growing stronger. We might add a third consideration: that the complexity and scale of the problems may have grown, as appears to be the case with climate change and with various forms of global conflict.

Accepting the plausibility of this picture of American decline raises the question of how to orient oneself to it. Each post-imperial reading of Mr. Obama has its preferred response to this question, and evaluates Mr. Obama's performance, or his significance, in light of this preference. For some the right response is eager acquiescence and adjustment to the new world, while for others the appropriate reaction is lamentation and perhaps resistance. Still others want to question the operating assumption, and suggest either that the decline is not as steep as it has been made out to be, or that what looks like waning power is really power taking new forms. As we saw in connection with race and with pragmatism, and as I'll discuss after a quick tour of the different positions, Mr. Obama has made enough noises and gestures in enough directions to invite each of these responses.

ANTI-IMPERIALISM

At one time, it was nearly as easy to find anti-imperialist readings of Mr. Obama as it was to find post-racialist readings. Robert Grenier, a former director of the CIA counter-terrorism center (under George W. Bush), gives a representative sample of the genre.

Here is how it looks in an article that appeared on *Al Jazeera* website:

> America's conception of its imperial role, and the imperial mindset which accompanies it, has sometimes caused America to badly overreach, as it did in Vietnam, arguably did in Iraq, and may yet be doing in Afghanistan. . . . That is precisely what Obama refuses to do in Libya, and properly so. . . . Obama now presides over a country badly over-stretched in its engagements abroad and in its fiscal arrangements at home. No longer able to sustain the role it assumed after World War II, it must somehow recalibrate both ends and means, both within its shores and beyond, before its current discomforts are transformed into a genuine decline.[29]

Quinn makes a similar point in his study of US "declinism," and in the study's title ("The Art of Declining Politely: Obama's Prudent Presidency and the Waning of American Power"). He acknowledges that US power has declined, insists that responsible statecraft requires a careful calibration of national aspirations in light of realistic judgments about the capacity to act, and praises President Obama for his "measured, cautious attitude towards the use of American power." He concludes: "the president's circumspect restraint [offers] a more appropriate complement to waning national power than the alternative."[30]

There are different ways to imagine Mr. Obama's role in this sea change in US politics. For people like the ones I encountered in South Africa, what matters most is that Mr. Obama is the son of a former colonial subject: that he is, in short, a *post*-colonial subject who was moved to replace an oval office bust of Winston Churchill with a bust of Martin King. For others the key is that he is a pragmatist, in at least one of the senses canvassed in the previous chapter. Free of the ideological commitments that drove his predecessor's global adventures, he can look soberly at global realities and govern himself, and the nation, accordingly, and intelligently. A third point of emphasis might have less to do with postcolonial inheritances or pragmatist predispositions than with cosmopolitan sensibilities. What matters here is that the simple stereotype of "east coast liberals" gets something right: they are, Mr. Obama is, more urbane and worldly than, say, Texas oilmen, which means that it is easier for him to see himself as a citizen of the world as well as of the US.

REALISM AND NOSTALGIC IMPERIALISM; OR, ANTI-ANTI-IMPERIALISM

While the anti-imperialist reading praises Mr. Obama's willingness to accept and adjust to America's waning fortunes, the nostalgic imperialist reading rails against them. For advocates of this form of post-historicism, history ends not by opening a door, in the liberating way that we associate with post-modernism, but by bringing down a curtain. Dinesh D'Souza may have provided the ur-text for this genre by devoting a *Forbes* article, entitled "How Obama Thinks," to the proposition that the president is an anticolonial zealot—in fact, "the last anticolonial."[31] But *The Economist*, a publication never accused of fawning over Mr. Obama, describes D'Souza's reading as "deranged" and as a "disgrace" and "an excrescence,"[32] so it may be better to look elsewhere.

There are ways to register dismay or disappointment over imperial decline without going to the lengths we see in D'Souza's piece. *The Economist* leads the way here again, pointing out that for a variety of reasons, the US "has lost an informal empire in Latin America but has yet to find a role."[33] Diplomatic historian and former state department advisor Aaron David Miller suggests that the presidency is no longer a site for heroic action and, thanks to the complexities of contemporary governance and of today's world, cannot be. His remedy? "We need to get over the greatness thing and stop pining for the return of leaders we can no longer have."[34]

These more modest attempts aside, articles by Charles Krauthammer and Robert Kagan more effectively occupy the conceptual and rhetorical space that D'Souza targeted. Kagan argues that the world has not changed as much as liberal internationalists like Obama (and Clinton, and Ikenberry, and so on) think it has. Global cooperation is a nice ideal but not a reality, and perhaps not a possibility; the reality is that great power politics, of the sort that the modern empires practiced, is still in play, and necessary.[35] Krauthammer, for his part, bridges the positions taken by Kagan and by D'Souza. Obama's America, he says, is not in decline but "in retreat—accepting, ratifying, and declaring its decline, and inviting rising powers to fill the vacuum." He shares D'Souza's diagnosis—the president is acting in the grip of "an adopted Third World narrative of American misdeeds"—but with an eye on Kagan's underlying concern with rational action in the sphere of great power politics.[36]

These anti-anti-imperialist approaches orient themselves to the post-historical impulse differently. For D'Souza, there is at least a hint of nostalgia for a world less concerned with equality and rights, a world that people like Obama have nearly ushered into oblivion. For Kagan, what might be coming to an end is the latest onset of the illusion that we've transcended great power politics. We come down with this affliction periodically, he says—before World War I, after World War II, at the end of the Cold War. And each time the world brings us to our senses. For him, Mr. Obama has not ushered in a post-imperial age—where "imperial" refers to the sort of expansive, influence-seeking and influence-exerting policies that marked US politics between 1945 and 1989 or so—no matter how much he and others act as if they have.

NEO-IMPERIALISM

The anti-imperialists and anti-anti-imperialists both accept that America is in decline and that President Obama has sought to accommodate this fact. They just disagree over how to take the news. Advocates for a neo-imperialist reading of the president, by contrast, argue that Mr. Obama has sought to shore up or reconstitute American imperial power.

Political scientist Adolph Reed, one of the president's most consistent and acerbic critics, makes the neo-imperialist case explicitly. "An Obama presidency," he explained before the 2008 election, "would further legitimize the imperialist orientation of US foreign policy by inscribing it as liberalism or the 'new kind' of progressivism."[37] For Reed as for a number of critics on the left, Mr. Obama is a kind of Trojan horse or Manchurian candidate. As many American progressives see it, this president functions essentially to make center-right or conservative policies more palatable to those who would otherwise oppose them, in part by combining (mostly) liberal social policies and post-racial optics with a willing embrace of, among other things, illiberal corporate agendas in trade and finance. For progressives who take race seriously, like Reed, the situation is even worse. For them Mr. Obama is also the US version of Amilcar Cabral's postcolonial "comprador" elite—those post-independence leaders who served as neo-imperial intermediaries, protecting the reconstituted relations of domination within which the nominally sovereign nations remained enmeshed.[38] Frantz Fanon marks out the relevant conceptual space in this description of the African post-colonial leader from *The Wretched of the Earth*:

> The people who for years on end have seen this leader and heard him speak . . . put their trust in this patriot. . . . But as soon as independence is declared, far from embodying in concrete form the needs of the people . . . the leader will reveal his inner purpose: to become the general president of that company of profiteers impatient for their returns which constitutes the national bourgeoisie.[39]

We have to re-read Fanon's "national bourgeoisie" as Reed's "black professional-managerial class," or as other commentators' "civil rights industry," but otherwise the argument is the same. The anti-imperial zealot that D'Souza feared is actually a neo-colonial intermediary in disguise. He gives US imperialism a brown face, even as US military adventures continue, and as US-led corporate interests continue to shape the world to their benefit.

Whether history comes to an end on this approach depends on what history one has in mind. For Reed, Mr. Obama sounds the death knell for twentieth-century liberalism, as he completes the Clintonian project of turning liberalism or progressivism into conservatism or neoliberalism. This is not anti-imperialism; it is the entrenchment of a certain kind of imperialism as political common sense, even for ostensible leftists. (As Reed puts it, liberals "don't mind imperialism; they just want [it] more efficiently and rationally managed. . . .") It is not the end of empire but the end of progressivism, which has been "transcended out of existence, along with race."[40]

POST-NATIONALISM

Like the neo-imperialist reading, the post-national approach sees the declinist claim as overblown. For advocates of this approach, the world has changed, to be sure, and the US does not, and cannot, exert its power in the way it once did. But to see this simply as a decline is to think too simply about power, and to ignore the persistence of something like imperial asymmetries in the distribution of social goods around the world.

I am using the rubric of post-nationalism to lump together a number of rather different thoughts, but all begin with some version of this insight from the eminent political theorist Sheldon Wolin. After noting the various late 20th-century manifestations of the post-historical impulse that I've put at the heart of this book, Wolin points out that

> [s]ignificantly absent was "post-political," and yet it might fit a phenomenon that some claimed as the most significant trend . . . the eclipse of the sovereign state. The emergence of globalizing corporations, the "internationalization" of culture, the European Union, international agencies such as the World Bank, and the growth of non-governmental organizations operating without much regard for national frontiers were interpreted as challenging the modern notion of the state as master within its boundaries. They might also be interpreted as questioning a conception of the political as contained within specific boundaries and the state as principally responsible for its care.[41]

Wolin goes on to argue that the US is no longer a modern nation-state. It has instead become something else, a new political form that he calls "Superpower." We once used this term to denote a particular kind of nation-state, one that has simply gotten itself in position to exert an unusually large influence over world affairs. But the US has taken this to such an extreme, and has changed so completely the mechanisms by which and purposes for which this influence gets brought to bear, that something new has actually emerged. Among the distinctive features of this new polity are "the increasing importance and involvement of corporations" in politics and policy, a concomitant "retrenchment" and downsizing of government *alongside* an increase in military expenditures, and, eventually, a willingness to embrace "more openly the idea of empire"—to "extend its sway" over more of the world by "establishing [military] bases . . . in exchange for financial aid and economic reconstruction."[42]

There is of course much more to Wolin's account, including his recent efforts to link it explicitly to the Obama administration, and to track the extension of imperial prerequisites into the domestic sphere, into the domain of civil liberties. But I invoke it here just to set the theoretical register for a general kind of argument, one that does not depend on his particular way of working it out. Political geographer Simon Reid-Henry develops a version of the position in an article for *New Statesman*, where he points out that Mr. Obama's "pragmatism" encourages him "to refine, rather than depart entirely, from Bush-era geopolitics." (He had previously described this as an imperial or "re-colonial" orientation to geopolitics, in an article on Guantanamo Bay.) What this means: striking deals to plant military outposts around the world, for the sake of "sustaining America's capacity to fight multiple fronts of a diffuse war on terror," and supporting "future and current military operations in Africa and the Pacific."[43]

The post-nationalist lesson for students of the Obama presidency is clear. As the neo-imperialist reading suggests, the alleged decline in US imperial power was an illusion. President Obama helped sell the illusion, perhaps intentionally, perhaps inadvertently—once again, the Eldridge principle applies: We don't know what Obama knows. Either way, he has presided over an unprecedented assertion of US-based power, and—going beyond the neo-imperial move as we developed it—he has overseen the diffusion of this power into unusual spheres. We hold enemy combatants in legal limbo without regard for international law or for our own laws; we push for trade regimes that erode the power of sovereign states to regulate and manage their economies; we assassinate people in distant lands— in foreign lands—without going to the trouble of declaring war or of pretending not to be involved, as in the days of old-fashioned espionage; and we support an overbuilt military apparatus that spills over into our domestic politics, both by distorting our politics with militaristic imperatives, as President Eisenhower foretold, and by recommending military techniques and material for use in domestic policing, as the clashes in Ferguson, Missouri revealed.

As before, there are various ways to relate these thoughts to the post-historical impulse. Perhaps the putative end of history was an illusion, a cover story that "Empire," in Hardt and Negri's version of the Wolin argument, uses to mask its transformation. Then again, perhaps the emergence of this new form does mark an end, and the onset of the moment that Wolin contemplates thinking of as "post-political." Most clearly, the curtain seems to have fallen on the agents of twentieth-century great power politics. States may still have roles to play, but they increasingly play them in a drama that is scripted by transnational or supra-national forces, like Superpower or Empire.

COMPLEXITIES, INTUITIONS, AND THE CHANGING SAME

I've identified four broad ways of thinking of Mr. Obama as a post-imperial figure, but it has of course been a provisional, somewhat idiosyncratic, and highly selective exercise. I've left out a number of topics, texts, and figures that could have figured prominently in this sort of discussion. And I've focused more on mapping the terrain than on taking a stand on the merits of one approach as opposed to another. The noncommittal nature of the discussion to this point is in part the reflection of an expository strategy—it was easier to tell the story that way. But it also, and more importantly, reflects my sense of the complexity of the issues.

It is much easier to assess the merits of post-racialist and pragmatic post-partisan readings of Mr. Obama than it is to evaluate the case for a post-imperial reading. The idea that pragmatist commitments interestingly shape the president's policy choices simply does not accord with easily accessible facts, unless "pragmatism" means something rather peculiar. And the idea that this president has ushered in or made visible a post-racial age—even working around his own refusal to endorse this claim, and even refining the claim into its most defensible form—just doesn't stand up to scrutiny. By contrast, the post-imperial reading admits of so many variations, and depends on so many judgments about political feasibility and desirability, that diffidence, at least in a discussion as space-constrained as this one, seems in order.

One way to get at the complexity of the post-imperial reading is to note that it never strays far from the domain that the other modes of post-historicism could, for the most part, pass lightly over. The post-racial reading was largely about what Mr. Obama *means*, and faltered when forced to take up questions about what he's done. Similarly, the pragmatist reading tried to focus on a version of the president—his earlier incarnations as a writer and as a candidate—that bore little relation to the man who as of this writing leads history's most powerful military. Post-imperialism, by contrast, is almost entirely about what the president, *qua* president, has done, or will do, or should do. Some versions of it, such as the post-colonial interpretation, might focus on what he means, on the symbolism, say, of having a son of Africa in the Oval Office. But then they run up against the same objections that undermined post-racialism: that the symbolism cuts multiple ways, and can make Mr. Obama an effective cog in the machinery of post-racial or neo-colonial racial projects.

To the extent that post-imperialism is about the actions of the president *qua* president, it requires that we take up knotty questions about political means and ends that I can't settle here. Is the world so dangerous that the assertion of state power must have more to do with warding off existential threats than with living up to lofty but unrealistic ideals? Or, by contrast, is it possible for global political actors to cooperate effectively in the construction of shared norms and imperfect but meaningful regulative practices? Are the particular exercises of power that define the Obama Doctrine, if there is one,[44] likely to be effective? Are they not just effective, but necessary? Or would other policies be more likely to solve our problems and do less damage to our ideals, even holding constant the policy's stated objectives? Is what looks like empire to some merely the rational determination to fill a global political vacuum, a vacuum that would otherwise get filled by actors with malign intent—or, at least, with designs that conflict with US national interests? Or is this determination more cynical than rational, and less about national interests than about less salutary motivations? We are suspended here not just between, say, Hobbesian and Kantian visions of the nature of and prospects for political life, but also between Cabral's Marxian anticolonialism and Ignatieff's paeans to liberal—"lite"—imperialism, and between, or among, a bewildering array of empirical details about the nuts and bolts of concrete policy interventions.

I can't settle these questions here, but I can gesture at the broad outlines of my intuitions about them. I am persuaded by constructivist accounts of the prospects for meaningful, multilateral global governance, without need of recourse to a great power or concert of powers standing in for, or standing up in the absence of, a Hobbesian sovereign.[45] I take seriously anti-militarist arguments that trace our foreign policy adventures to interests—chief among them, economic interests—other than, and typically at odds with, anything we could plausibly call "the national interest." I believe Mr. Obama is sincere when he calls for global cooperation, with the US as one nation among many in a community of moral (if not military or economic) equals. But I think he also accepts that global cooperation must unfold on terms that are consistent with the global order largely as it stands, which is to say, an order that is marked by what Pogge calls "radical inequality," and that has its roots in an "historical process"—colonialism—"that was pervaded by massive grievous wrongs."[46] Mr. Obama freely acknowledges these historic wrongs, just as he does in relation to US racial politics. But also as in the US case, he is committed to a framework for intervention that begins by taking the outcome of this wrongdoing largely as a *fait accompli*, and that only then seeks to attend to the people on the bottom of the relevant distributions—and then only insofar as doing so is consistent with the needs of corporate elites. *But* I recognize also that there are different routes to this posture: that it might be the issue of rational calculations about what's possible given existing constraints rather than of considered ethical convictions. And, as I keep saying, I don't know what Obama knows.

With these intuitions in place, I find myself reacting to the post-imperial readings of Mr. Obama much the way Waldo Martin reacted to Hollinger's post-racialism. Yes, one wants to say, the world has changed in the ways that the declinist reading of US power suggests. But these changes are complicated, and pull in different directions, and do not—absent an explicit commitment to the comforts of empire as such—entail that US power is in any sort of dire tailspin. As the neo-imperial and post-national readings at their best mean to suggest, the changes are a kind of "changing same," with power extruded from one realm—the old balance of power, great game politics of mighty nation-states—surfacing in another realm—in the politics of regional and transnational forces, working across and around and through sovereign boundaries and institutions to advance *and contest* the interests of various global actors, beginning with but not limited to corporate elites.

At the same time, while something like imperial power persists and adjusts to new conditions and exploits new openings, things *have* genuinely changed. Yes, one wants to say, by any objective measure, the US is no weakling, and global resources are distributed in ways that eerily mirror imperial arrangements. The former colonial powers are in fact clustered at the top of global indices of development and well-being, while former—and current—possessions cluster at the bottom. What's more, one can plausibly argue, as Pogge does, "that, by shaping and enforcing the social conditions that foreseeably and avoidably cause the monumental suffering of global poverty, we"—the beneficiaries of the extant arrangements, the people at the top of the neo-imperial distributions—"are harming the global poor," and doing so in ways for which we should be held accountable.[47] And military might—in the form of sovereign armies and of private contractors—is in fact spread across the globe, at least in part to protect the reigning distribution of opportunities and resources. Nevertheless, the world is complex enough, the conditions and consequences of the exercise of human agency, individual and collective, are convoluted enough, that it is too simple to say that empire owes its resurgence either to the machinations of global cabals or to power flowing like electricity through (over? around?) the ruins of prostrate, no longer sovereign states.

All of these complexities may in fact be the best warrant for invoking the idea of the post-imperial. The ambivalence inherent in the "post-" makes two things clear. We are not where we once were: the US is not the British Empire in 1885. But we remain haunted by what we once were, and by what we don't yet know how not to be.

To ask where Mr. Obama fits into all this is to add yet another level of complexity to the discussion. I agree with Quinn that "seeking to discern the definitive soul of this president's worldview" may just be unproductive, both because of who he is—the blank screen for other people's projections—and because of what the presidency is, with its unceasing demands for concrete action in situations of competing, often incommensurable goods. So instead of sifting through Mr. Obama's public pronouncements and comparing them with, say, the actions of his representatives at multilateral trade negotiations, I will join Quinn in adopting "a humbler aim, highlighting one significant element" of Mr. Obama's relationship to post-imperial possibilities.[48] This will have less to do with what Mr. Obama has done as a policymaker than with what he means, and what the first lady means.

I'll pursue this aim with the help of resources that tend not to figure prominently in the kinds of debates that I've spent the middle portion of this chapter engaging. This will mean setting aside the political theorists, international relations scholars, and other commentators on geopolitics, and turning back to Said's colonialist structures of attitude and reference. And it will mean returning to the psychocultural terrain that Cullwick and Munby so ostentatiously inhabited.

THE PRESIDENCY'S TWO BODIES

One moral of the Cullwick and Munby story is a central proposition of post-colonial theory: that modern imperialism was, in addition to everything else it was, a remarkable mechanism for producing particular kinds of human subjects. (There are other morals, beginning with the remarkable diversity of forms that human erotic experience can take.) There are many ways to unpack the workings of this mechanism; there are in fact too many, and they develop the implications of too many different sets of theoretical commitments, to do justice to any of them here. Suffice it to say that theorists of intersubjectivity and recognition from Hegel and Freud to Mead, Fanon, De Beauvoir, and bell hooks have made clear, in a variety of ways, that the formation of human identities and self-conceptions is a complicated, transactional, dialectical process, unfolding at the point where individual choices intersect with cultural resources, social encounters, and power relations. Hegel's master-slave parable, Sartre's peeping tom, Fanon's "Look, a Negro!", and Laura Mulvey's reflections on the male gaze in film all tease out dimensions of this process.

Thinking specifically about the constitution of colonial subjects puts the dialectics of subject formation into the context of the specific axes of social differentiation that empire mobilized to do its work. Colonial subjects were encouraged to imagine themselves as particular kinds of people, specifically in relation to the imperial project, and therefore specifically in relation to the ideas of race, gender, sexuality, and economic life that justified imperial hierarchies. Cullwick and Munby show the lengths to which this process of self-imagining can go, while also clearly indicating which clusters of meaning, which structures of attitude and reference, which possible selves, the imperial enterprise made available to them.

Remember the options that Cullwick's performances revealed. She could be a grubby laborer, with the centrality of grubbiness to the exercise highlighted in a variety of colorful ways. She could be a non-white male slave, or a nursemaid caring for a child. Or, most saliently for current purposes, she could be a middle-class white lady, the proper female partner in a respectable bourgeois couple.

More precisely: She could *pretend* to be a middle class lady, as this performance was more distant from her sense of herself than the performances that constituted her as a working woman. She wasn't a lady, and didn't want to be one, because being a lady meant being demure and dainty and idle, which is to say that it meant traversing class boundaries that she preferred not to traverse, and comporting herself in ways that did not interest her. But because she was white—because, contemporary philosophical race theorists invite us to say, she possessed a thin racial endowment consistent with thick ascriptions of whiteness—she could *pass* or, as McClintock says, cross-dress as a lady when it was convenient or pleasurable to do so.

These various identity options presented themselves to Cullwick at a moment when modern ideas about domesticity and femininity, about bourgeois respectability, about labor and servitude, and about citizenship and foreignness were all taking shape. And all of these were intertwined with convictions about superior and inferior racial types. They were, in fact, articulated with these convictions, in the double-barreled sense of "articulate" that various post-Enlightenment traditions recommend to us: both expressed through, as one articulates a statement, and linked but with scope for independent movement, as with an articulated bus.[49] Modern imperialism was bound up with firm ideas about who counted as civilized or savage, as citizen or foreign other, as respectable or squalid. These ideas were in turn bound up with assumptions about race, about sexuality, and about gender. And this cloud of meanings tended to resolve itself into a handful of semi-stable configurations. In the clearest cases, the respectable, temperate white lady stood opposed to the squalid, promiscuous, black or brown female; and the white, masculine, sovereign citizen stood opposed to the dark, brutishly male, savage subject.

What all this, finally, has to do with the Obama presidency: We've seen that colonial structures, both material and discursive, continue to shape contemporary life. Explaining how this works in material terms is a task best undertaken in close proximity to the data and the evidence, which is not the sort of thing philosophers are typically good for. So it will pay us to focus here on the discursive structures, which haunt the current occupants of the White House as surely as they haunted Sarkozy in Senegal.

I've focused to this point on President Obama, principally on what he means to his observers, to a lesser degree on what he has said and done, mainly while in office. I have said almost nothing about the fact that he occupies a role in an institution, and that the institution of the presidency is defined in part by a peculiar blending of distinct roles. US presidents are chief executives, ceremonial heads of state, and, nowadays, high-end celebrities. But they are also, quite prominently, heads of families, and these families are supposed to mean something to the nation. Every election cycle, as the punditry and political classes begin to feel out possible candidates, we entertain questions about the optics of the potential candidate's family—whether his or her partner passes muster with the voters, whether the family life seems genuine; how he or she will overcome being single, if by some tragic accident, the unfortunate aspirant happens not to have a publicly declared life partner certified by the state.

The cultural significance that we assign to the presidency still apparently requires that we obsess over that clearly archaic but still resonant part of the institution that we call "the First Lady." We are now more comfortable with the prospect of a woman being president than we have ever been before. But so far all of the presidents have been men, and all of the female occupants of the White House have been wives or daughters. (The centrality of family life to the presidency, our collective determination to link political leadership to publicly sanctioned expressions of sexual desire and gender identity, is evident in the fact that we've not yet taken seriously the thought that the first family might have a gay or lesbian couple at its core.) And the wives have been forced, for the sake of their husbands' political survival, to take on a daunting, perhaps impossible role. As one scholar puts it, these women "face insuperable obstacles arising out of expectations that they are to represent . . . a single universally accepted ideal for US womanhood."[50]

It is not inconsequential that this ideal is rendered as the first *lady*, a rubric that, as Hortense Spillers points out, conjures images of "lace and crinoline."[51] This is the same ideal that Hannah Cullwick grappled and played with, resounding with the same overtones of domesticity and idleness and bourgeois respectability. But in a fascinating inversion of Cullwick's situation, in which phys-iognomic whiteness could, for a time, overcome the agent's own preferences, self-concept, and social location, Michelle Obama's claim to middle-class femininity, a claim that should have been bolstered in the public mind by her ivy league degrees and her successful career as a lawyer, was overwhelmed by her blackness, which is in part to say, by her body.

Black femininity has always been a problem in the US, as towering figures from Anna Julia Cooper to Angela Davis have pointed out. In her germinal text from 1892, *A Voice from the South*, Cooper points out that there is an "all-leveling prejudice . . . in America which cynically assumes that 'A Negro woman cannot be a lady.'"[52] This prejudice still persists, as Lisa Thompson points out in her study of the symbol of "the black lady," which focuses on the public meanings of figures like Anita Hill and Condoleeza Rice. Thompson explains that middle-class black women have historically faced, and still face, considerable pressures to "counter negative stereotypes" with a rigorous performance of feminine identity, relying "heavily on aggressive shielding of the body; concealing sexuality; and foregrounding morality, intelligence, and civility. . . ."[53] (Reconciling blackness with the ideal of the lady is not the only way to make sense of or room for black female experience and agency. It is, moreover, clearly not an unproblematic way of doing this. It is, however, the way that bears most directly on the topic of this chapter, in light of which I will bracket the important objections to the heterosexist and classist dimensions of the project.)

Due in part to this history of the politics of the black lady, Michelle Obama's arrival in Washington is in some ways as remarkable a development as her husband's election. After all, the couple did win the presidency, which means that they were able to overcome lingering vestiges of Cooper's "all-leveling prejudice" among members of the voting public. And this happened despite Mrs. Obama's clear departure from the canonical ways of performing respectable black womanhood. She is, for one thing, not a demure, retiring presence. It has always been clear that she is an independent, self-directed agent, even as she focuses on "mothering her two small children, serving as a role model for women, and evincing a sense of style missing from Washington for decades."[54] She has in addition been willing to be seen as a physical presence. She dances, exercises, and plays sports in public; and she wears daring fashions that precisely do not "aggressively shield the body."

Mrs. Obama's physical presence is important because this is a particularly vexed dimension of identity performance for black women. Feminist thinkers and activists have long sought to complicate the thought that women are nothing but bodies or objects, and to overcome anxious associations of the feminine with corporeality, with the heteronomous demands of blood and flesh. As Susan Bordo points out, though, a black woman faces "a triple burden of negative bodily associations":

> By virtue of her sex, she represents the temptations of the flesh and the source of man's moral downfall. By virtue of her race, she is instinctual animal, undeserving of privacy and undemanding of respect. . . . But the legacy of slavery has added an additional element. . . . For in slavery her body is not only treated as an animal body but is *property*, to be taken and used at will.[55]

This triple burden motivates and informs the politics of the black lady, and leads to its historic concern with shielding and concealment. It also makes all the more remarkable Mrs. Obama's fashion adventurousness, and all the more predictable the public fascination with her body.

As Mrs. Obama became a more prominent public figure, her body became subject to increasingly invasive and critical scrutiny. As one commentator points out, "[n]ewspapers and bloggers"— eventually joined by congressmen, and popular talk radio hosts— "often focused on specific parts of [her] body, especially her buttocks."[56] There was, in addition, considerable media discussion of whether she was overweight, and of the frequency with which she dressed in ways that left her arms—her *muscular* arms, it was always pointed out—bare. Of course, women in the public eye are almost always subjected to this sort of scrutiny; and the increasing fitness-orientation in hegemonic ideals of female beauty has a great deal to do with the focus on Mrs. Obama's arms. But the fascination with the buttocks, and with female strength, and with the danger of obesity tracks familiar ways of scrutinizing black women's bodies that go back to the saga of colonial subject Sara Baartman, the so-called "Hottentot Venus." The persistence of these colonial associations speaks to the capacity of these meanings to continue to haunt us, even in the present.

We see similar associations at work in relation to Mr. Obama. His body and physical presence also became the focus of attention, in ways that evoke long-standing practices of reducing black men to brute physicality. But more interesting for current purposes is the way the president has been consistently represented by certain of his critics as essentially and irredeemably "other." Tesler and Sears conclude from their empirical study of voter attitudes "that Obama is not just evaluated as an African American but as someone who exemplifies the more primitively frightening out-group status of 'otherness.'"[57] The president's opponents, beginning most clearly with John McCain and Sarah Palin, have routinely stressed his father's Kenyan origins and his "foreign-sounding" name, and thereby activate anti-Muslim attitudes in their target audiences. The remarkable persistence of the "birther" movement, whose members are convinced that Mr. Obama is not a US citizen, is one sign of this phenomenon. Another sign: the frequency with which one used to hear charges that the president—a center-right politician whose signature domestic policy is a repurposed Republican health care plan—is a socialist or even a terrorist.

The idea of the other as an inassimilable, alien danger—or, as one insightful theorist of race has it, a representative of a strange and unruly population[58]—is one of the mainstays of imperial culture. It marked the clearly imperial phase of US continental expansion, as indigenous peoples, peoples annexed with Mexico and Hawaii, religious minorities like Jews and Catholics, and immigrants of all kinds—from Asia and even, for a time, from problematic white lands, like Ireland and Italy—were at various times depicted as obstacles to the maturation and progress of American civilization. It is an obvious feature of our contemporary politics of immigration, which might itself be described as a function of imperial blowback. (Like this: When you invite people in distant lands to think of the metropole as their homeland or otherwise as a vital part of their lives, like French colonial subjects raised on stories beginning with "We Gauls . . .," then those people will eventually want to *come* home.) And, strangely, or not so strangely, it now constitutes part of the political minefield that the president of the United States has to navigate just to do his job.

CONCLUSION

It is difficult to settle on a single story to tell about the prospects for the president as a post-imperial figure. The evidence is equivocal at best, both in the domain of geopolitics and in the domain of cultural meaning. I suggested above that the best move is to invoke Baraka's idea of the changing same and to proceed swiftly either to a study of details or, if the details are elusive or time and space are short, to a provisional examination of considerations that might nevertheless reward some preliminary reflection.

In the area of international relations, the complexities make empirical detail vital, and make the idea of empire in some ways a crude instrument for mapping the flows and configurations of global power and influence. The anti-imperialist and the anti-anti-imperialist readings of the Obama administration are right to hold that the world has changed, and that US global ambitions have changed with it. But the post-nationalist and the neo-imperial readings are also right to hold that US power, or the power of elites or interests interestingly tied to the US, remains largely intact, and has even been heightened in some ways. Mr. Obama seems to have played his part on both sides, helping both to restrain US ambitions and to extend the reach of what Wolin calls "Superpower."

Similarly, in the area of cultural meanings, the unrelenting swirl of otherwise inexplicable associations around Mr. and Mrs. Obama recommends different ways of taking up the question of empire.

The Obamas clearly accept that their political prospects are tied to their performances in a neo-colonial domestic drama, a drama built around idle bourgeois ladies (with avocations but no jobs, with status but no inherited titles) and masterful, sovereign husbands (equal parts CEO and military commander, and breadwinner). At the same time, though, their performances are complicated by the determination of their audiences, and of the relevant narrative structures, to resist having people like them play these roles. The lady's idleness and domestic distractions were, in their original forms, made possible by colonial labor and resources; and, as Cooper notes, she is not supposed to be black, even now. Similarly, the husband's mastery and self-possession were defined, in their original forms, by opposition to the colonial subject and the slave; and he is not supposed to be the Other, even now. If Tesler and Sears are right, if the election of 2008 was in fact the most racially polarizing election we've seen, and if race is just one strand in the complex intersectional tapestry of colonial subject formation, then the Obama administration's claim to post-imperial status may rest most securely on its neocolonial reinscription of imperial structures of attitude.

NOTES

1 I am grateful to Jonathan Shaheen for this reference, and for the translation.

2 Charles F. Peterson, *Dubois, Fanon, Cabral: The Margins of Elite Anti-colonial Leadership* (Lanham, MD: Lexington Books, 2007), 107.

3 Barack Obama, *The Audacity of Hope* (New York: Three Rivers Press, 2006), 11.

4 *See* Article 1 of the 1933 Montevideo Convention on the Rights and Duties of States, 49 Stat. 3097; Treaty Series 881, accessed December 19, 2014 at http://avalon.law.yale.edu/20th_century/intam03.asp#art1; see also www.cfr.org/sovereignty/montevideo-convention-rights-duties-states/p15897

5 Liah Greeneld, *Nationalism: Five Roads to Modernity* (Cambridge, MA: Harvard University Press, 1993); Isaiah Berlin, *The Proper Study of Mankind: An Anthology of Essays*, Henry Hardy and Roger Hausheer, Eds. (New York: Farrar, Straus and Giroux, 1998), 553–604.

6 From Jennifer Pitts, "Political Theory of Empire and Imperialism," *Annu Rev Polit Sci*, 13 (2010), 211–235. Downloaded from www.annualreviews.org, p. 213, citing C.J. Calhoun, F. Cooper, K.W. Moore, and Social Science

Research Council (U.S.), *Lessons of Empire: Imperial Histories and American Power* (New York: New Press, 2006), vi.

7 Reinhold Niebuhr, *The Irony of American History* (Chicago, IL: University of Chicago Press, 2010), 2, 37.

8 Edward Said, *Culture and Imperialism* (New York: Vintage-Random House, 1994), xxii.

9 Wenzlhuemer, Roland J. "Empire, British," *Encyclopedia of Western Colonialism since 1450.* Ed. Thomas Benjamin. Vol. 1. Detroit: Macmillan Reference USA, 2007, 359–369. *Gale Virtual Reference Library.* Web. December 19, 2014; *World and Its Peoples, Vol. 2: France, Andorra, Monaco* (Tarrytown, NY: Marshall Cavendish, 2010), 214.

10 Edward Said, *Culture and Imperialism* (New York: Vintage-Random House, 1994), 9, emphasis added.

11 Said 9, emphasis in original.

12 "Intersectionality" appears here as a placeholder for accounts of the way different axes of social differentiation and oppression conspire to shape social life and individual experience. Intersectionality theory is one approach, but not the only one and perhaps not the best one. *See* Kristie Dotson, "Knowing in Space: Three Lessons from Black Women's Social Theory," *Labrys* 22 (2013), accessed December 29, 2014 at www.tanianavarroswain.com.br/labrys/labrys23/filosofia/kristieok.htm; and "Making Sense: The Multistability of Oppression and the Importance of Intersectionality," in *Why Race and Gender Still Matter: An Intersectional Approach*, Eds. Namita Goswami, Maeve O'Donovan, and Lisa Yount (London: Pickering and Chatto, 2014), 43–57.

13 Said, xxiii.

14 Padraig Carmody, *The New Scramble For Africa* (Malden, MA: Polity, 2011), 3.

15 W.E.B. Du Bois, *The World and Africa* (1946; New York: International Publishers, 1965), 58.

16 Angus Maddison, *The World Economy: A Millennial Perspective* (Paris, France: Development Centre of the Organisation for Economic Co-operation and Development, 2001), 19, accessed December 19, 2014 at www.keepeek.com/Digital-Asset-Management/oecd/economics/the-world-economy_9789264189980-en

17 Adam Hochschild, *King Leopold's Ghost* (New York: Mariner-Houghton Mifflin, 1999), 259.

18 "The Four Dollar Stella," Numismatic Guaranty Corporation, accessed December 20, 2014 at www.ngccoin.com/gallery/stella.aspx; real dollar values calculated at MeasuringWorth.com, accessed December 20, 2014 at www.measuringworth.com/uscompare/relativevalue.php

19 Adam Hochschild, *King Leopold's Ghost* (New York: Mariner-Houghton Mifflin, 1999), 233.

20 Thomas, Dominic Richard David, *Africa and France: Postcolonial Cultures, Migration, and Racism* (Bloomington: Indiana University Press, 2013), 13.

21 Thomas, 89, citing Nicolas Sarkozy, "Speech at Chiekh Anta Diop University," Dakar, Senegal, July 26, 2007. Partial video accessed December 19, 2014 at www.youtube.com/watch?v=s32eInxqubw

22 Diadie Ba, "Africans Still Seething Over Sarkozy Speech," *Reuters* September 5, 2007, accessed December 19, 2014 at http://uk.reuters.com/article/2007/09/05/uk-africa-sarkozy-idUKL0513034620070905

23 McClintock, Anne P. (2013-01-28). *Imperial Leather: Race, Gender and Sexuality in the Colonial Contest* (Kindle Locations 219–221). ACLS Humanities E-Book. Kindle Edition.

24 McClintock, 132–133, Kindle location 2694.

25 Kathryn Huges, "Review of *Love and Dirt: The Marriage of Arthur Munby and Hannah Cullwick*, by Diane Atkinson," *The Guardian* (UK), January 18, 2003, accessed December 19, 2014 at www.theguardian.com/books/2003/jan/18/featuresreviews.guardianreview2

26 McClintock, 136–137 (Kindle Locations 2750–2752).

27 McClintock, 143 (Kindle Locations 2868–2870).

28 Adam Quinn, "The Art of Declining Politely: Obama's Prudent Presidency and the Waning of American Power," *International Affairs*, 87:4 (2011), 803–824, 805.

29 Robert Grenier, "Obama Striving For Post_Imperialism," *Al Jazeera*, April 5, 2011, accessed October 18, 2014 at www.aljazeera.com/indepth/opinion/2011/04/20114573424979413.html

30 Adam Quinn, "The Art of Declining Politely: Obama's Prudent Presidency and the Waning of American Power," *International Affairs*, 87:4 (2011), 803–824.

31 Dinhesh D'Souza, "How Obama Thinks," *Forbes* September 9, 2010, accessed December 22, 2014 at www.forbes.com/forbes/2010/0927/politics-socialism-capitalism-private-enterprises-obama-business-problem.html

32 "How D'Souza Thinks; Obama Derangement Syndrome," *The Economist* (Online), September 13, 2010, accessed December 22, 2014 at http://search.proquest.com/docview/851243881?accountid=13158; "Against D'Souza," *The Economist* (Online), September 30, 2010, accessed December 22, 2014 at http://search.proquest.com/docview/850843216?accountid=13158

33 "The Post-Imperial Void," *The Economist*, 411, no. 8886 (May 10, 2014): 34–24, accessed October 18, 2014 at http://search.proquest.com/docview/1523677154?accountid=13158

34 Aaron David Miller, "We Have Reached Peak President," *Foreign Policy*, October 14, 2014, accessed October 21, 2014 at http://foreignpolicy.com/2014/10/14/we-have-reached-peak-president/

35 Kagan, Robert, "The Perils of Wishful Thinking," *The American Interest*, Jan, 2010, pp14–16, accessed December 22, 2014 at http://search.proquest.com/docview/224657767?accountid=13158

36 Charles Krauthammer, "The Fruits of Weakness," *National Review Online*, May 21, 2010, accessed December 22, 2014 at www.nationalreview.com/articles/229800/fruits-weakness/charles-krauthammer

37 "Where Obamaism Seems to be Going," Adolph Reed, Jr., *Black Agenda Report*, July 16, 2008, accessed July 28, 2008 at www.blackagendareport.com/content/where-obamaism-seems-be-going

38 Amilcar Cabral, "Presuppositions and Objectives of National Liberation in Relation to Social Structure" (1966), in David McLellan, Ed., *Marxism: Essential Writings* (New York: Oxford University Press, 1988), 392–408, 400.

39 Frantz Fanon, *The Wretched of the Earth*, Constance Farrington, trans. (New York: Grove Weidenfield-*Presence Africaine*, 1963), 166.

40 Reed, ibid.

41 Sheldon Wolin, *Politics and Vision, expanded edition* (Princeton, NJ: Princeton University Press, 2004), 559.

42 Wolin, 560–561.

43 Simon Reid-Henry, "Coming Soon to Obama's Backyard," *New Statesman*, 138 (August 3, 2009), 31, accessed February 5, 2010 at http://search.proquest.com/docview/224312753?accountid=13158; Reid-Henry, Simon, "Exceptional Sovereignty? Guantánamo Bay and the Re-Colonial Present," *Antipode*, 39:4 (2007), 627–648. Academic Search Alumni Edition, EBSCOhost (accessed December 22, 2014).

44 Aaron Blake and Chris Cillizza, 'The Obama Doctrine', *Washington Post*, March 29, 2011, accessed December 22, 2014 at www.washingtonpost.com/blogs/the-fix/post/the-obama-doctrine/2011/03/29/AFbqHqtB_blog.html

45 *See* John Ruggie, "Reconstituting the Global Public Domain," *European Journal of International Relations*, 10:4 (2004), 499–531; Peter Haas, "UN Conferences and Constructivist Governance of the Environment," *Global Governance*, 8 (2002), 73–91; John Ruggie, "Foreword," in Thomas Weiss and Ramesh Thakur, *Global Governance and the UN* (Bloomington: Indiana University Press, 2010), xv–xx.

46 Thomas Pogge, "Real World Justice," *The Journal of Ethics*, 9 (2005), 29–53, 38.

47 Pogge, 33.

48 Quinn, 814.

49 Stuart Hall, "Assembling the 80s—The Deluge and After," in *Shades of Black*, Eds. David A. Bailey, Ian Baucom, and Sonia Boyce (Durham, NC: Duke University Press, 2005), 1–20.

50 Karlyn Kohrs Campbell, "The Rhetorical Presidency: A Two Person Career," in *Beyond the Rhetorical Presidency*, Ed. Martin J. Medhurst (College Station, TX: Texas A & M University Press, 1996), 191.

51 Hortense Spillers, "Views of the East Wing: On Michelle Obama," *Communication and Critical/Cultural Studies*, 6:3 (2009), 307–310, 307.

52 Anna Julia Cooper, "Womanhood: A Vital Element in the Regeneration and Progress of a Race," *The Voice of Anna Julia Cooper*, Eds. Charles Lemert and Esme Bhan (Lanham, MD: Rowman and Littlefield, 1988), 70.

53 Lisa Thompson, *Beyond the Black Lady* (Chicago, IL: University of Illinois Press, 2009), 2.

54 Mary L. Kahl "First Lady Michelle Obama: Advocate for Strong Families," *Communication and Critical/Cultural Studies*, 6:3 (2009), 316–320, 316.

55 Susan Bordo, *Unbearable Weight: Feminism, Western Culture, and the Body* (Berkeley, CA: University of California Press, 1993), 11.

56 Margaret Quinlan, Benjamin Bates, and Jennifer Webb "Michelle Obama 'Got Back': (Re)Defining (Counter)Stereotypes of Black Females," *Women and Language*, 35:1 (2012), 119–126, 121–122.

57 Michael Tesler and David Sears, *Obama's Race: The 2008 Election and the Dream of a Post-Racial America* (Chicago, IL: University of Chicago Press, 2010), Kindle Locations 159–160.

58 Falguni Sheth, *Toward a Political Philosophy of Race* (Albany, NY: SUNY Press, 2009).

Conclusion

On August 9, 2014, in Ferguson, Missouri, a young black man named Michael Brown was shot and killed by a white police officer named Darren Wilson. The circumstances of the shooting were unclear, with different witnesses describing the situation differently. What was clear was that Brown was unarmed, that the situation had escalated from a starting point that in no way called for the use of lethal force, and that this was the latest in a string of similar incidents—incidents in which black people lost their lives at the hands of police or security forces in suspicious situations.

The distressing familiarity of the events of August 9 led to an equally familiar, and equally distressing, cycle of reaction and counter-reaction. First came protest, police response, outrage at the scale and vigor of the police response, and outrage at the disruption of public order by the protesters. Then, after the county prosecutor failed to secure an indictment to try the police officer for possible criminal violations, there was more outrage, this time at the inability or unwillingness of the state's juridical machinery to accommodate the protester's concerns. This led to more protests, in Ferguson and elsewhere around the world; to more resentment of the protests; and to a renewed police response.

As the crisis escalated and the protests spread, public debates about how to understand the underlying pattern—of race-related, police-involved killings—both spread and intensified. For some the explanation was simple. Blacks commit more crimes, police are empowered to use force to stop crime, and appeals to racial victimization needlessly obscure this simple fact, thereby complicating the work of maintaining social order. For others the situation was more complex, and involved systemic anti-black bias converging with overdeveloped state capacities for surveillance and violence. For still others, including many observers outside the US, the situation revealed a creeping ethical rot in the heart of ostensibly democratic states, as evidenced by the close parallels between political repression in places like Palestine and what was happening in the putative land of the free.

The various responses to Ferguson tended to agree on at least one thing: there was something deeper at stake than the life of one man and the career of another. This was an irreducibly political situation, in the expansive sense of the political that goes beyond jockeying for votes in campaigns and legislatures. This was about the ethical conditions for community life, and the ethical implications of the way this life expresses itself in conjoint action. It was about race, and security, and freedom, and justice, and democracy, and history, and, it turned out, about money—about white-run municipalities treating black populations as revenue sources, and using police powers to extract the rents. It was about many, if not all, of these things at once, and also about dismay at the way these things, in these combinations and forms, still bedevil us—still, that is, after such milestones as the prophetic witness of Martin King, the race-transcending genius of Oprah Winfrey and Michael Jackson, the quiet distinction of Condi Rice, and, above all, the historic ascent of Barack and Michelle Obama.

As with other race-related controversies during the Obama administration, there was considerable interest in just how the president would address the situation. Even his most ardent supporters realized that he had to walk a fine line. On the one hand, he had to address concerns raised by his core constituencies, concerns that had the added urgency of implicating basic issues of democratic equality. On the other hand, though, he had to avoid giving in, or giving the appearance of giving in, to "special interests." He had to make clear, as he sometimes put it, that he was the president of the United States of America, not of black America. But he also, many people thought, had to assure US citizens that all of their lives matter in the eyes of the state. So he had to do something.

Mr. Obama's responses sounded familiar themes from his other engagements with racial politics, and seemed not to reassure many people at all. On August 18, shortly after the initial round of protests, he wearily commented on the Ferguson situation after providing an update on developments in Iraq. He acknowledged that tensions were high and announced that the attorney general would visit Missouri and otherwise monitor the situation. He then called on the protesters to remain peaceful and reminded the police to respect the rights of free speech and assembly. On November 24, after the St. Louis County grand jury declined to indict Officer Wilson, he held a press conference squarely on the Ferguson situation. He called for calm and urged people to respect the rule of law, but acknowledged that "a deep distrust exists between law enforcement and communities of color," and that this is so in part because "the law too often feels as if it is being applied in discriminatory fashion." There are real problems, he noted, and "communities of color aren't just making these problems up." But we should focus on moving forward and on solving the problems, which "won't be done by throwing bottles."[1]

As the president was speaking, social media commentators took great interest in the optics of the moment. Many television news outlets showed the president's address in split screen. One side of the screen showed Mr. Obama, his trademark "cool" appearing to shade into something like resignation, straining, if that's the right word, to find words that were adequate to the situation. The other side showed dramatic images of protesters and police apparently locked in conflict, amid swirling tear gas and burning flames.

Two days later, on November 26, 2014, the radical intellectual Cornel West said in an interview, "I think Ferguson signifies the end of the Age of Obama."[2]

I've introduced Professor West's comment here for two reasons. First, it captures some of what I've been after in this book, though from a different angle, and I want to use this new angle to summarize my aims here from that new perspective. Second, West raises political considerations that bear directly on my project but that I've mostly tried to bracket. I want to make clear just how I've tried to orient this book to the work of politics and ethics, and why I've done it this way.

What might it mean to say that the Age of Obama is at an end? West's answer to this is bound up with a particular reading of the Obama moment, and with a scathing critique of the president based on this reading. As West sees it, Obama supporters thought they'd hired someone to turn the page on militarism and financialization and the surveillance state, but instead got "a Wall Street presidency, drone presidency, mass surveillance presidency. . . ."[3]

I have tried to stop short of focusing on particular policy prescriptions and ethical commitments of the sort that West identifies with the Obama moment, in order to focus instead on the broader sense of the moment *as* a moment. Mr. Obama rose to prominence on the strength of a message of hope and change—of hope *for* change. It didn't particularly matter that there was, and had to be, considerable disagreement about what this change would look like. Even many of Mr. Obama's critics thought that history was about to shift. They agreed that he represented the end of something and the birth of something new. They simply viewed this prospect less as something to hope for than as something to dread.

This, to me, is the broader significance of talking about an Age of Obama: We, many of us, thought that a new day was dawning, for good or ill, even when it was unclear what the novelty would bring. For the people who found this prospect appealing, it looked like this: We would get beyond race, and in the process would get over our attachment to the register of social life that required Hollinger's abhorrent solidaristic protocols. We would get beyond partisanship, and in the process discover, or rediscover, the room to maneuver that opens with the pragmatic preference for problem-solving over ideology. We would get beyond empire, and realize possibilities for global governance, cosmopolitan citizenship, and international cooperation that had been suppressed by the rigid frameworks of the late imperial world.

The Obama moment was, in this sense, about endings and new beginnings. It was about venturing, hopefully *or* fearfully, into the world that becomes possible once the old ways are abandoned. And this moment comes to an end when it becomes clear that the endings it promised are not in the offing: that the old ways are still in force, and that the new beginnings are not what we thought.

My interest in this broader point about the Obama moment is only one of the reasons I've been keen to conduct the argument at a quite general level, with as little recourse to social criticism as I can manage. The second reason is methodological, and was aired to some degree in Chapter 2. Mr. Obama is a public official, significant not just as a symbol of the nation or repository of national aspirations, but also as a part of the apparatus that generates and executes public policy. A fully developed criticism of someone like that requires attending to the details of the policy interventions, and exploring with care the social-theoretic and ethical assumptions that frame the interventions. I've not had the space to do much of that work, and so have tried to bracket the kinds of criticisms that would depend on it.

It occurs to me now, though, that what strikes me as bracketing social criticism might strike readers as evading it, and that I can say more without running afoul of my various reasons for saying less. I pledged above to avoid ethical pronouncements and policy prescriptions, but there is some space between these enterprises, and social criticism is one of the enterprises that occupies this space. So I'll take a moment to extend my earlier, truncated gestures and expand on the provocations that have already made their way into the argument to this point. Hopefully this will make them feel less like stray complaints than like the argument that waits beneath this one, peeking through every now and again, awaiting its turn to break through.

I have two broad, social-critical worries about Mr. Obama as a political figure. As I've said earlier in the book, these are not worries about his performance as a politician or as a policymaker. As I'll explain in the next section, they are not worries about his comportment as a moral agent. And as I probably should have said in related contexts before now, they are not attempts to deny his remarkable gifts or his undeniable attractiveness as a public figure. My worries have to do with Mr. Obama's impact on, or his enactment or embodiment of, the prospects for political agency in the current moment. Mr. Obama strikes me as an emblem for the narrowing and constriction of our politics, and as an agent, whatever his intentions in this regard, for the acceleration and intensification of these processes.

My concerns begin where Mr. Obama himself often does, and where stories about him often do: with the idea of compromise. In his fine account of Mr. Obama's rise to the presidency, *The Bridge*, David Remnick writes the following:

> What Obama understood from the start of his political career was that a purist, an anti-machine politician . . . might gain a stronger foothold on the path to Heaven but would never advance far on the path to power. . . . [T]o be a successful politician you had to make a few compromises along the way. Obama rarely failed to make them.[4]

To which one of course feels compelled to ask: Is the acquisition of power self-justifying, or might the compromises undertaken in pursuit of power at some point undermine the ends to which the power might have been put? In a slightly different spirit, one might also ask whether what looks like compromise is really a tardy acquiescence to an unfortunate status quo. Or, as a famous line from Malcolm X encourages me to put it: If you plunge an eight-inch knife into my back, pulling it out six inches will feel like more of a compromise to you than it does to me.[5]

I mean here to be generalizing a worry that came into view in the discussion of pragmatism. Real politics in a democracy—politics as a dimension of human social life, not as a game for beltway elites and TV pundits—can't be conciliation and compromise all the way down. The compromise must serve some end. We would have to argue about what that end is, and whether people ostensibly committed to the philosophic doctrines of liberalism and pragmatism have the resources to consistently pursue anything called an end. Let's say that the end is as thin as Rawls and other liberal theorists suggest, involving no more—not to say that this is a small thing—than sustaining the conditions under which people with different visions of the good can peaceably live together as free and equal citizens. Even so, compromise in service of this goal is compromise for the sake of more than mere compromise. There must be a point in every policy debate at which the conciliatory impulse might lose its purchase on us, if it gives away something that matters too much. And if we plot a line through those points in relation to key policy questions in this administration, we end up with what looks for all the world like a neat protective boundary around the interests that dominate contemporary formal politics, especially in the financial and health insurance sectors.

It is possible to read this fealty to entrenched elite interests as itself a necessary compromise, or as a realistic acquiescence to the constraints on contemporary governance. This acquiescence is supposed to be the price of admission to the space where real work gets done in formal politics. But reading it in this way requires that we forget the tendency of formal politics to get routinized, and that we forget *how those routines forget* how to get truly important things done. Abolitionism and the Civil Rights movement, to use only the examples that seem closest to the president's heart, were not matters of political routine or of politics as usual. These and other movements show the importance of the people that formal politics wants to silence, and of the causes and aspirations that it typically wants to compromise away.

The response at this point is of course to point out, rightly, that the president is not, cannot be, an activist. There is and must be a gap between formal politics and political activity more broadly construed, and willingness to compromise is one of the things that mark this gap. (Other markers include, sometimes, an unending devotion to the deep-pocketed donors who will fund the next campaign.) An apocryphal line from Franklin Roosevelt famously locates our topic here. *That's a fine idea*, Roosevelt was reputed to have said when a critic offered an alternative to one of his policies: *now go make me do it*. Which is to say, go mobilize the demos to put pressure on the machinery of governance, because that's what keeps the machinery accountable to the people. Which is therefore to say: we need the disorderly activists to agitate and shift the public sense of what's possible and desirable. This is what happened when the abolitionists shifted the ground beneath more diffident politicians, like Lincoln, who were less interested in racial equality or black humanity than in preserving the union. But this division of labor works, the argument concludes, only if the government is populated by figures who, like Lincoln or FDR or, in the case of civil rights, Lyndon Johnson, will answer, however tardily or reluctantly, when the people call. And those figures must compromise to acquire and keep their positions, and to get things done while they are there.

The problem with this view in relation to Mr. Obama brings us to the second of my two social-critical worries about Mr. Obama's presidency. As a reading of figures like FDR and Lincoln—and, for that matter, of Mr. Obama's not-so-guilty pleasure, Ronald Reagan—this compromiser-in-chief approach ignores the role that the occupant of the Oval Office can play in supporting the demos, framing the issues, and shifting public opinion. We saw in Chapter 2 that Mr. Obama soared into office on the strength of a massive and massively inspired constituency, and that, once in office, his team worked tirelessly and successfully to domesticate this constituency. This is a clear abdication, a repudiation, of the role the administration might have played in helping to mobilize and remain in conversation with the people to whom it should be saying, *go make me do it.*

This selective indifference to the presidency's role in vernacular democratic practice has also, it appears, largely led Mr. Obama to ignore the presidency's potential as a bully pulpit—a potential he knows and on occasion actualizes better than most of his predecessors. He has routinely declined to bring his considerable oratorical and writerly gifts to bear on the task of articulating a grand ethical vision—whatever "grand" comes to for whatever sort of pragmatist some people think he is. Nor does he often bring those gifts to bear on the work of reframing the difficult debates that bind our politics, despite his frequently stated desire to undo this binding. He will spring into this sort of action on occasion, most often in relation to the racial issues that he managed with such adroitness during his initial presidential run. (Hence what one progressive blogger wrote of the president's 2015 speech at the Edmund Pettus Bridge: "Obama Gives Another Greatest Speech Ever, This Time In Selma,"[6]) But he does this quite rarely, especially in relation to what many people—including his own speechwriters, on occasion —regard as the other real issues, in addition to race, that face the country. This happens so infrequently, in fact, that it's easy to credit the thought that on some issues, some important issues, some important issues that Mr. Obama claims to care about, like economic inequality, climate change, and public education, he is, as the Clintons once argued, all talk.

Saying any more in the social-critical spirit I mean to be adopting here would require transcending that spirit, and would require the sort of detailed policy argument that I've pledged not to attempt. So think of this section as a down payment on a longer argument that I'll make on some other occasion. I offered this gesture, as I noted above, in the hope that it would clarify the distance between the judicious bracketing for which I'm aiming, and the kind of simple evasion that it might resemble.

I've tried to keep the argument of this book at some remove not just from policy questions, but also from narrowly moral questions. What I mean: I once explained the basic argument of the book, brackets and all, to a colleague. She worried that I'd seemed keen to bring moral critique to bear on Mr. Obama, but had shied away each time. "Why not just say that he's a bad guy?" she asked. I take it that she was asking something like this: Why not say that he is personally blameworthy for his willingness to play the role I've pointed to in my social-critical gesture above? Why stop with worrying, as I say above, that he is an emblem for certain unfortunate social dynamics? Why bother to say that he is the agent of certain processes while then remaining agnostic or, in any case, silent, on his culpability for or viciousness in this role?

I have three reasons for declining to argue for Mr. Obama's wickedness or perfidy. The first, also sounded in Chapter 2, has to do with the sequencing of ethical argumentation. To demand of Mr. Obama that he be different presupposes that he can be: that the demands of his office are not such that the people occupying it have to act more or less as he does. This presupposition may be true, but it is not obviously true. I think the presidency could be different, and that the US could be; but I've not had room to make this case, and simply gesturing at it would render the argument that I am trying to make needlessly inaccessible to readers who don't share my assumptions. When I can say more about my views on, say, heterodox economics and on the prophetic possibilities of the presidential bully pulpit, then I'll be in a better position to engage in ethical evaluation.

In the meantime, I've tried to excavate, explore, and, where necessary, criticize certain influential beliefs about the Obama presidency. Many beliefs worth exploring in this way did not make their way into this discussion, and many of the ones that did appear here might well have appeared more profitably in a different kind of discussion. But it seemed to me that the idea of the post-historical presidency provided a kind of framing that would make clear, as one account of the philosopher's job has it, how things, in the broadest sense, hang together, in the broadest sense.[7]

A second reason to refrain from moralizing about the president is that moral evaluation is highly contextual. In order to reflect productively on Mr. Obama's character, I would need to know a great deal more about the specific, concrete, daily challenges that he faces. Unfortunately, the presidency is not simply a nearly impossible job, but a fairly mysterious one, one that few people can really claim to understand. In light of that, it is entirely possible that Mr. Obama is performing admirably under conditions that I can't fathom. I do wish the governmental apparatus behaved differently, but to collapse that into a wish that this one man behave differently, and into the corresponding judgment that he is vicious or blameworthy because he doesn't, is almost surely to overstate the power of the office, to misunderstand the nature of leadership in large organizations, and to pretend that I have the god-like capacity to peer into his soul, and into the workings of his organizations, from afar. Consider this a corollary to the point I borrowed from Michael Eldridge in Chapter 2: Not only do I not know what Obama knows, but I don't know what he intends, or contends with, or desires, or believes.

I do, however, know what Mr. Obama says, at least in public, and I know that these words don't always track the policies his administration pursues, allows, or proposes. This sounds like more support for the "he's a bad guy" view, but instead leads me to a third reason for steering clear of this sort of moral criticism. Angela Davis puts the point I have in mind quite effectively. "The problem of the presidency" she explains, "is not primarily a question of deceit—most people, regardless of their political affiliations, and regardless of their level of education, take for granted the fact that politicians lie and deceive." What then *is* the problem of the presidency? Davis is thinking here of George W. Bush, who was reelected, she argues, "because of the panic generated by the September 11 attacks and because of the ease with which we were all entranced by the images and rhetoric of nationalism. . . ." She concludes: "I am more concerned about the ease with which this moral panic emerged than I am about presidential dishonesty and deception."[8]

Davis suggests that we should focus less on the person in the president's office than on the broader structures that underwrite the office and that frame its functioning. Doing this requires that we locate and inhabit an analytical space for thinking through, among other things, the meaning of the presidency, and the meanings that get mobilized around it. This is the spirit in which I have tried to engage with Mr. Obama. I have tried to focus less on the president's character than on the wider discursive conditions that enable the approach to governance and to political life that he seems to represent.

All my attempts at bracketing notwithstanding, it is difficult to resist the impulse to moral evaluation, or to avoid receiving the arguments I have made as anything other than steps toward a moral complaint. They surely constitute an *ethical* complaint, in a sense of these terms that distinguishes the ethical, with its openness to the political, from the narrower but included category of the moral, with its focus on such things as individual obligations and praising and blaming. But I have tried to refrain from moralizing about Mr. Obama.

I do not, however, mean to rule moral criticism out of bounds. It is a register we routinely occupy in dealing with our fellows, irrespective of whether we have good grounds for doing so, irrespective of the gaps, empirical or epistemic, between what we actually know about them and what a responsible evaluator would need to know. This impulse becomes all the more irresistible when we contemplate what Machiavelli called "great personages"— those figures whose excellence, as Emerson, puts it, raises the credit of all the citizens.[9] For these reasons, I doubt that Mr. Obama would bristle at the overtones of moral evaluation. He is, after all, the man who wrote these words before his first presidential run:

> Recently, one of the reporters covering Capitol Hill stopped me on the way to my office and mentioned that she had enjoyed reading my first book. "I wonder," she said, "if you can be that interesting in the next one you write." By which she meant, I wonder if you can be honest now that you are a U.S. senator.
> I wonder, too, sometimes.[10]

NOTES

1 Barack Obama, "Remarks by the President After Announcement of the Decision by the Grand Jury in Ferguson, Missouri," accessed December 26, 2014 at www.whitehouse.gov/the-press-office/2014/11/24/remarks-president-after-announcement-decision-grand-jury-ferguson-missou; video available at www.c-span.org/video/?322940–1/president-obama-statement-ferguson-grand-jury-decision

2 "Interview with Cornel West," CNN, November 26, 2014, quoted in Kirsten West Savali, "Cornel West Is Right About Obama and Ferguson," *theroot.com*, December 2, 2014, par. 2., accessed December 26, 2014 at http://us.cnn.com/video/data/2.0/video/world/2014/11/26/wrn-ferguson-race-america-cornel-west-intv.cnn-ap.html

3 Cornel West, "The State of Black America in the Age of Obama," *Salon.com*, October 5, 2014, accessed December 26, 2014 at www.salon.com/2014/10/05/cornel_west_the_state_of_black_america_in_the_age_of_obama_has_been_one_of_desperation_confusion_and_capitulation/?utm_source=facebook&utm_medium=socialflow; David Remnick, *The Bridge* (New York: Alfred A. Knopf, 2010), Kindle location 8124.

4 David Remnick, *The Bridge* (New York: Alfred A. Knopf, 2010), Kindle location 8124.

5 "If you stick a knife in my back nine inches and pull it out six inches, there's no progress. If you pull it all the way out that's not progress. Progress is healing the wound that the blow made." Malcolm X, "TV interview after 90-day moratorium" (March 1964), video available at https://www.youtube.com/watch?v=cReCQE8B5nY, accessed March 20, 2015.

6 Lambert Strether, "Obama Gives Another Greatest Speech Ever, This Time In Selma," *Naked Capitalism*, posted on March 8, 2015, accessed March 25, 2015

at www.nakedcapitalism.com/2015/03/obama-gives-another-greatest-speech-ever-time-selma.html?utm_source=feedburner&utm_medium=email&utm_campaign=Feed:+NakedCapitalism+(naked+capitalism)

7 Wilfrid Sellars, "Philosophy and the Scientific Image of Man," *Empiricism and the Philosophy of Mind* (London: Routledge & Kegan Paul, 1963), 1–40.

8 Angela Y. Davis and Eduardo Mendieta, *Abolition Democracy: Beyond Prisons, Torture, and Empire: Interviews with Angela Y. Davis* (New York: Seven Stories Press, 2005), Kindle Edition, Kindle Locations 625–627, 627–629, 636–637.

9 "The knowledge, that in the city is a man who invented the railroad, raises the credit of all the citizens." Ralph Waldo Emerson, *The Complete Works of Ralph Waldo Emerson, Centenary Edition Vol. IV: Representative Men: Seven Lectures* (1850; Boston: Houghton Mifflin, 1903–1904), 4:31.

10 Barack Obama, *The Audacity of Hope* (New York: Random House-Crown, 2006), 12.

Made in the USA
Monee, IL
22 December 2021